FÉILE VOICES AT 30

Memoirs of West Belfast Community Festival, Féile an Phobail

Edited by

Feargal Mac Ionnrachtaigh and Michael Pierse

Féile Voices at 30: *Memoirs of West Belfast Community Festival, Féile an Phobail*
edited by Feargal Mac Ionnrachtaigh and Michael Pierse

This book is typeset by SPRINTprint, Ireland.

e-mail: feargalenright@hotmail.com

First printed July 2018

ISBN: 978-1-78605-065-6

Printed in Dublin, Ireland by SPRINTprint

This project is generously supported by funding from the Arts and Humanities Research Council.

ACKNOWLEDGEMENTS

Ba mhaith linn buíochas mór a ghabháil le réimse leathan de dhaoine a thug cuidiú, tacaíocht agus comhairle leis an tionscadail seo a chur i gcrích. Firstly, we would like to thank all the memoir contributors who gave up their time to recount their experiences on paper. Most of them and upwards of 30 others, who also deserve a mention, also kindly agreed to take part in interviews for our oral history archive and for that we are eternally grateful. We would like to recognise the AHRC for funding the Féile research project and Margaret Topping, Órla Nic Ruairí, Seán Ó Treasaigh and Lorraine Browne from Queen's University for their collaboration. We have depended, from the beginning of the project, on our partnership with Féile an Phobail, who not only funded the memoir publication, but have also played a supportive role in the project. In particular, Kevin Gamble, Kevin Morrison, Gráinne Maskey, Harry Connolly and Tony McDonagh have given very kindly of their time. All proceeds from this book will go towards sustaining the impact of Féile in local communities.

We want to give particular mention to Claire Hackett from the Dúchas archive who has worked with us from the outset, whilst, Phil Scraton, and Bill Rolston and Danny Morrison have also been on hand to lend advice and support. When gathering and compiling the archival material and photographs, we were supported by various people including Ciarán Cahill from Springhill Community House, Tony from Fáilte Feirste Thiar, Bill Rolston, Seán McKernan, Mal McCann, Seán Murray, Chrissie Mhic Siacais, Jimmy McMullan, Gerard 'Mo Chara' Kelly, Veronica Brown, Máirtín Keenan, Anthony Neeson and Brónach Ní Thuama from the Belfast Media Group. We would also like to give special thanks to Deaglán Ó Mocháin and Dearcán Media, who produced the documentary on the history of the Féile and who kindly agreed to give us access to their many hours of additional footage. Gerry Kelly and Benil Shah from Orpen Press deserve special praise for their efficiency, accuracy and patience during the publication process.

Some friends such as Fearghal Mac Bhloscaidh, Ciarán Mac Giolla Bhéin and Niall Enright have kindly read drafts of the manuscript while Máirtín Mac Gabhann supported us on the Irish-language text.

We would like to thank our families and especially our wives, Maura and Brenda, for their patience and unswerving support throughout. Go raibh maith agaibh uilig.

CONTENTS

Contents

CONTRIBUTORS

Ciarán De Baróid – *'From little acorns: the Upper Springfield Community Festival'*

Ciarán was born and raised in Cork and later moved to Ballymurphy in West Belfast having cut short international travels. He became a youth leader in the BTA (Ballymurphy Tenants' Association) and helped organise the 1973-4 Upper Springfield festivals. He later worked as Manager of the Upper Springfield Resource Centre and played a central role in campaigning on social justice issues in the area. He was centrally involved in setting up the Springhill and West Belfast festivals. Ciarán is author of the acclaimed book, *Ballymurphy and the Irish War* (2000, Pluto Press) and the personal memoir *Down North-Reflections of Ballymurphy and the early Troubles* (2010, Ogham Press). Ciarán recently retired after spending ten years as Project Officer with the Community Foundation for Northern Ireland.

His piece details the forerunner festival to Féile an Phobail, which took place in the Upper Springfield Area in 1973 after a period of intense warfare and hardship.

Jimmy McMullan – *'From humble beginnings'*

Jimmy, also known as 'Teapot', was born and raised in West Belfast and was imprisoned in Long Kesh where he was a republican prisoner during the Blanket Protest of 1976-81. Upon his release, he played a central role in prisoner solidarity campaigns, including organising numerous high-profile fundraising concerts. Jimmy would bring this experience to Féile an Phobail as a founding member of the first organising committee and a key figure during the festival's formative years.

Jimmy's piece outlines the battle to organise the first festival in 1988 and organisers' attempts to persuade Sinéad O'Connor to play.

Aidan McAteer – *'In memory of Seán Lavery'*

Aidan was born in Derry and moved to Belfast as a child. A lifelong republican activist, he spent six years imprisoned in Long Kesh prison before returning to

West Belfast, where he became active in the development of Sinn Féin. He was a founding member of the first West Belfast Festival committee in 1988 and remained active until the mid-1990s before he began to work full-time with the Sinn Féin negotiating team in the developing peace process. He now manages the Sinn Féin Assembly team at Stormont.

Aidan's piece details the rationale and power behind the first Féile. He dedicates the piece to Seán Lavery, who was killed during the 1993 Féile on the night that the first republican rally made it to Belfast's City Hall.

Deirdre McManus – 'Bród'

Another West Belfast native, Deirdre became active in community development in the late 1970s. She worked for many years in the Falls Community Council and was a founder member of the original Féile an Phobail committee, playing a key role in its formative years. When Féile eventually received project funding in 1995, Deirdre became the first festival Director when the Féile was based in Cultúrlann McAdam Ó Fiaich. Here, Deirdre was central to many of the key developments at Féile during that period. She is now based in South Armagh and works in Bunscoil an Iúir.

Deirdre's piece, 'Bród' ('Pride') considers the challenges and highlights of those early formative féiltí.

Micheál Mac Giolla Ghunna – 'Féile: where humanity can flourish'

Micheál was born and raised in North Belfast and moved to Fermanagh in early childhood. Upon returning to the city, he attended Queen's University Belfast where he became involved in many political and social justice campaigns. Micheál worked as part of the original Féile an Phobail organising committee and also became embroiled in the campaign against political vetting, when Irish language group, Glór na nGael, lost their funding. He would later be imprisoned in Long Kesh between 1990-97, where he played a key role in educational development, including the formation of an Irish-language wing, Gaeltacht na Fuiseoige, the development of a prisoners' magazine, *An Glór Gafa*, and the foundation of a prisoner drama group, which produced plays that were showcased during Féile an Phobail. Micheál now works as a teacher in Coláiste Feirste, where he is Vice-Principal.

Micheál's piece refers to his role in the first Féile and his work as a political prisoner developing radical political theatre approaches that would be showcased during Féile.

Contributors

Gerry Adams – '*Féile an Phobail – 30 years a-growing*'

From the Ballymurphy area of West Belfast, Gerry became politically active in his teens and was later imprisoned in Long Kesh in the early 1970s. A leading figure in the Republican Movement, he became President of Sinn Féin in 1983, a position he held until recently stepping down at the end of 2017. An author of numerous autobiographical books, Gerry was also the MP for West Belfast for almost 20 years, is currently, since 2011, a TD for County Louth in Leinster House, and is a founder-member of the first Féile an Phobail committee.

Gerry's piece focuses on the politics of Féile as the community alternative to destructive rioting. He gives mention to many of the unsung heroes who built Féile from the bottom up.

Fachtna Ó Ceallaigh – '*By hook or by crook*'

Fachtna is a music promoter from Dublin and former manager of world-renowned Irish singer Sinéad O'Connor. He also managed bands and musicians such as the Boomtown Rats, Bananarama, Clannad, Dónal Lunny, Leslie Winer and Morrissey. He was a music consultant for Universal Music and occasional DJ at RTÉ Radio and various festivals such as 'Body and Soul'. Fachtna met the Féile organisers before the first festival in 1988 and has helped and supported their work since then.

Fachtna's memoir recalls his first encounter with the founding Féile organisers and the impression the festival left on him thereafter.

Tom Hartley – '*From political activist to tour guide and author*'

Tom was born and raised in West Belfast and became a leading member of Sinn Féin from the mid-1970s. A central player in the Sinn Féin peace strategy, he was later elected to Belfast City Council and became the city's Mayor in 2008-9. He played a lead role in developing the highly popular historical bus tours and graveyard tours during Féile, while also engaging in political outreach to unionism by using history events as a means for community reconciliation. Tom is now an active historian and author, having written two books emanating from this work, *Written in Stone – the History of the Belfast City Cemetery* (2006) and *Milltown – the History of Belfast Written in Stone* (2014).

Tom's piece recalls his own journey from political activist to Féile tour guide and how his interest in Belfast cemeteries, enthused by his popular walking tours, inspired him to document this history.

Tommy Holland – '*From Bramble Folk to Boyzone*'

Tommy was centrally involved in the development of the Springhill Community Festival, which was a mainstay of the Féile for well over a decade. He has played a central role in many community development projects in West Belfast, including the Upper Springfield Development Trust, on whose board he still sits. Tommy has been Féile board member for many years and remains central to the local community events committee. He now manages the Upper Springfield Resource Centre.

Tommy's piece details the early experiences of the Springhill Festival and how it would shape and transform him as a community activist.

Seán 'Johnboy' Ó Muireagáin – *'Ceiliúradh a dhéanamh don chomóradh'*

Rugadh Seán i Londain agus tógadh i mBaile Uí Mhurchú é in Iarthar Bhéal Feirste. D'fhoghlaim sé Gaeilge sna déaga malla agus bhí baint aige le forbairt phobail sa cheantar fríd Ionad Áiseanna Frank Cahill. Chiallaigh seo go raibh baint aige leis na hiarrachtaí chun tús a chur leis an chéad naíscoil agus bunscoil Ghaelach sa cheantar mar a bhí Naíscoil agus Bunscoil an tSléibhe Dhuibh. Chuidigh Seán fosta le bunú Chlub Eachtra, an chéad chumann óige Gaeilge sa cheantar, agus bhí baint aige, chomh maith, leis an Chultúrlann sna luathbhlianta, nuair a d'fhorbair sé mar ionad siamsaíochta agus ceolchoirmeacha. D'oibrigh Seán ar an fho-choiste imeachtaí ó shin agus bunaitheoir atá ann d'Fhéile an Earraigh i 2004. Oibríonn sé go lánaimseartha anois do Chomhairle na Gaelscolaíochta agus tá clú air fosta mar gheall ar an fhilíocht Ghaeilge s'aige.

Labhraíonn píosa Johnboy fán dóigh ar athraigh an Fhéile an saol don aos óg nuair a bunaíodh í.

Born in London and raised in West Belfast, Seán learned Irish in his late teens and became involved in community development through the Upper Springfield Resource centre. This led to his involvement in the local festival committee and also to his active involvement in the setting up of Ballymurphy's first Irish-medium nursery school and primary school, Naíscoil and Bunscoil an tSléibhe Dhuibh. Seán also helped establish the Club Eachtra Irish-language youth club and was involved in the early years of An Chultúrlann, when it developed as a venue for the emerging Irish language social/concert scene. Seán has worked on the Féile an Phobail Events Committee ever since and was a founder of Féile an Earraigh in 2004. He now works full-time for the Council for Irish Medium Education (Comhairle na Gaelscolaíochta) and is an acclaimed Irish-language poet.

Seán's piece explores how Féile changed things for young people in West Belfast.

Eilish Rooney – *'Being at Féile: resistance and reconciliation'*

Eilish was born and raised in the Ballymurphy area of West Belfast. Having returned to further education in the 1980s through Des Wilson's Springhill House, she then went on to become a community educator herself, in Springhill

House and then Conway Mill Education. Eilish has also spent many years as a community activist, with active involvement in grassroots community education projects and with particular focus on women's empowerment and community development. She is currently Senior Lecturer in the University of Ulster Community Development degree.

Eilish's piece discusses her Féile highlights over the years. She argues that it represents a unique combination of resistance and reconciliation.

Jim Gibney – 'Féile – politics and craic'

From the Short Strand area of South-East Belfast, Jim is a lifelong republican activist. Imprisoned on three separate occasions, while in jail Jim played a prominent role in the Anti-H Block campaign and the development of Sinn Féin in Belfast. He has been a member of the Féile an Phobail Debates and Discussions Committee for over twenty years. Jim currently manages the Sinn Féin constituency office in Twinbrook and writes a column in the *Irish News*.

Jim's piece discusses how Féile's 'open door' policy became a means of political outreach and reconciliation in the formative years of the Peace Process.

Joby Fox – 'Féile – the real change-makers'

Born and raised in West Belfast, Joby became interested in music in his early teens. He later moved to London and joined the renowned band the Bank Robbers, who were signed by EMI records in 1983. Two years later, Joby left the band to form a new group, Energy Orchard, which landed a five-album deal with ECA in 1988. It was Energy Orchard's first single, 'Belfast', penned by Fox, which really kicked off the band's career. Because of the West Belfast connection, the band played Féile a couple of times during the early years. After leaving the band in 1991, Joby returned to Belfast and became more directly involved in Féile, offering his expertise and utilising his contacts to organise concerts and attract music acts. Joby still works as a singer-songwriter and is also involved in Belfast's independent Folktown Market.

Joby's piece focuses on that first Féile and playing there with Energy Orchard.

Laurence McKeown – 'Film Festival – From West to Belfast-wide'

Hailing from Randalstown in County Antrim, Laurence joined the IRA at 17 years of age and completed a life sentence as a republican prisoner in Long Kesh, where he also survived 71 days on hunger strike in 1981. There, he was central to the development of collective education programmes, creative writing and theatre productions with the prisoner community. Upon his release, Laurence completed a PhD that produced a sociological study of the republican prisoner community in Long Kesh. This was published as a book, *Out of Time*

(Beyond the Pale), in 2001. Laurence also co-wrote a feature film about the Hunger Strike, *H3*, which was released in the same year. He was a founder member of the West Belfast Film Festival, which started out with Féile in 1996 before later becoming the Belfast Film Festival. Laurence now lives in Dundalk and works as a playwright.

Laurence's piece focuses specifically on the background and establishment of the West Belfast Film Festival and its subsequent growth and development into an important event in the Belfast cultural calendar.

Fergus Ó hÍr – *'Féile – an uprising of community creativity, talent, pride, positivity and resistance'*

A leading member of the Civil Rights Movement and founder member of People's Democracy (PD) in the late 1960s, Fergus was also centrally involved in the foundation of the Relatives' Action Committees and the Anti-H Block movement. A native of West Belfast, he was elected in 1981 as a PD representative for the area on Belfast City Council. A schoolteacher by profession, Fergus was later to become Principal of the North's first Irish-medium secondary school, Meánscoil Feirste, and he would play a key role in the school's high-profile 1990s campaign for recognition from the Department of Education. Fergus went on to become full-time manager of Belfast Irish-language radio station, Raidió Fáilte, where he still works.

Fergus's piece discusses the brutal context of the Féile's inception and recalls some of its key highlights, including the singer/songwriter folk evenings that he played a central role in organising.

Caitríona Ruane – *'Bringing colour, beaming children's faces and sunshine to the darkest of days'*

Hailing from County Mayo, Caitríona studied in America on a professional tennis scholarship, which she subsequently left to travel in South America. There, she became involved in solidarity and humanitarian work in Nicaragua. Caitríona later moved to West Belfast and helped establish the Committee for Research and Development (CRDA), which carried out human-rights based research and advocacy work. She worked as Director of Féile from 1996 until 2001, when she left her post to work on the 'Free the Columbia Three' campaign. In 2003, Caitríona would be elected as a Sinn Féin MLA for South Down in the Northern Ireland Assembly, and after four years there she took on the role of Minister of Education, before spending a period on the Policing Board of Northern Ireland. Caitríona retired from politics in 2017.

Caitríona's piece discusses her key Féile highlights.

Contributors

Máirtín Flynn – *'I thank Féile for the days'*

A West Belfast native, Máirtín began his working life as a volunteer with Féile in his early teens. Having trained on the Triple FM radio station, he worked for many years there managing advertising and fundraising. Máirtín also worked on high-profile Féile concerts and as a stage manager with Dubbeljoint theatre group on plays that were showcased as part of the festival. His experiences with Féile helped him gain employment for a period with the BBC. He now works for the Northern Ireland Housing Executive.

Máirtín's piece refers to his introduction to Féile as a teenager during the scorching hot summer of 1995. He describes how he went on to work with Féile Radio, which in turn shaped his own career.

Claire Hackett – *'Irish, queer and equal?'*

Claire is originally from Co Tyrone but has lived in Belfast since studying here in the late 1970s and early 1980s. Having played a key role in the women's movement and gay rights activism in Belfast, Claire later worked in the Upper Springfield Development Trust, as a training mentor in its URBAN initiative, where she began taking her own show on Triple/Féile FM. She later led the Falls Community Council's Dúchas oral history project, which collates and archives the social and political history of the conflict in Belfast. Through this work, Claire also led the cross-community EU-funded Pieces of the Past project which saw the Shankill's Women's Centre and Shankill Library co-organise and co-host historical talks and exhibitions during Féile an Phobail. Claire currently sits on the Féile Debates and Discussions group, which organises the Féile summer school.

Claire's piece recalls the ground-breaking event hosted by Féile in 2000, 'Irish, Queer and Equal', which was one of the first high-profile gay rights events/discussions ever held in West Belfast.

Jake Mac Siacais – *'Éacht phobail – ceiliúradh pobail'*

Is as Béal Feirste do Jake agus daoradh é chuig cásanna na Ceise Fada idir 1975 agus 1977, áit ar fhoghlaim sé Gaeilge. Go gairid ina dhiaidh do bheith scaoilte saor, ghabhadh arís é agus daoradh chuig na Blocanna H é idir 1977 agus 1982. I rith na tréimhse seo, d'imir sé ról lárnach i bhForbairt na Gaeilge i measc na gcimí sa phríosún. Nuair a scaoileadh saor é, bhí sé iontach gníomhach i saol na Gaeilge agus san fhorbairt phobail i mBéal Feirste — Féile an Phobail san áireamh. D'oibrigh sé mar fo-eagarthóir i Nuachtán Bhaile Andarsan agus Lá sular ghlac sé lena ról reatha mar stiurthóir ar an áisínteacht forbartha Gaeilge, Forbairt Feirste, a imríonn ról lárnach i bhforbairt na Ceathrún Gaeltachta.

San alt leis, tagraíonn Jake do bhuaicphointí na Féile dar leis agus an bhaint a bhí aige leo.

Jake is from Belfast and was sentenced to the cages of Long Kesh, where he learned the Irish language, from 1975 to 1977. Shortly after his release, he was re-arrested and sentenced to the H-Blocks of Long Kesh, where he was imprisoned from 1977 to 1982. During this period he played a central role in Irish language development in the prison. Following his release, he has been very active in Irish language and community development in Belfast. He worked as a sub-editor with the *Andersonstown News* and *Lá* newspapers before taking up his current post as Director of Belfast Irish language development agency, *Forbairt Feirste*, which is centrally involved in the development of the Gaeltacht Quarter in West Belfast.

In his piece, Jake recalls his Féile highlights and charts his own involvement in Féile.

Terry Goldsmith – 'Moving mountains and meadows'

Terry is a well-known environmentalist from West Belfast. He is a founder member of Friends of the Bog Meadows, which spearheaded the 1980s campaign to preserve the Bog Meadows from destruction. Terry was also a founder member of the Black Mountain Environmental Group, which campaigned against quarrying on the mountain and provided educational tours and resources to schools and members of the local community.

In his piece, Terry considers environmental activism and how it connected with the aims and vision of Féile an Phobail.

Christine Poland – 'If we can do it, so can you'

Native to West Belfast, Christine started her involvement in community development through the Falls Womens' Centre. She was also central to JustUs women's theatre group, which emanated from Féile, and wrote many of the scenes in plays like *Just a Prisoner's Wife* (1995) and *Binlids* (1997). She would later work full-time for Féile, as a training development co-ordinator providing accredited courses for young people. She remains active in developing community training programmes and is a qualified alternative therapist.

Christine's memoir recalls her experiences as a writer, playwright and active member of the JustUs Community Theatre group.

Bill Rolston – 'The D&D group'

Another West Belfast native, Bill studied in Belfast and the USA. As an academic activist in the University of Ulster, he conducted ground-breaking sociological research in the early 1980s on the nature of political imprisonment in the north of Ireland and the effects of repressive legislation. Bill co-established the radical, independent publishing company, Beyond the Pale, which gave voice to the many community struggles and hidden histories that attracted little interest from mainstream publishers. The foremost authority on political wall murals in the North, Bill has published extensively on this form of visual art which is also integral to the Féile story. A founder member of the West Belfast Economic Forum, Bill also co-authored the Obair Report on employment discrimination in West Belfast. He has spent many years on the Féile Debates and Discussions (D & D) Sub-Committee and now chairs the summer school. A former Director of the Transitional Justice Institute in the University of Ulster, Bill is now an Emeritus Professor at the university.

Bill's memoir charts his involvement with the Féile D & D group and discusses some of the highlights of this celebrated summer school.

Carol Moore – 'Féile: a way of life'

Carol was born in Ardoyne in North Belfast but was raised in the west of the city. Having spent many years working on republican prisoner solidarity campaigns, she moved to Féile an Phobail in the mid-1990s, as an administrative assistant on an Ace scheme. Carol later became a central organiser at Féile, spearheading the Draíocht children's festival. She eventually became Director of Féile, from 2001 until 2005, and now works full-time for Sinn Féin as Human Resources Manager.

Carol's piece discusses her own journey with Féile, from voluntary adminis-trator to high-profile director, and how Féile shaped her personally.

Veronica Brown – 'My days in Féile radio'

Having been brought into contact with Féile an Phobail through an Ace scheme, Veronica would become centrally involved in Triple FM and subsequently play a key role in managing the station between 1996 and 2004. She co-ordinated a highly successful media and radio skills training programme for young people in West Belfast. She now works full-time in the Upper Springfield Development Trust's Job Assist programme.

Veronica charts her role as Triple FM and later Féile FM radio manager.

Stephen McGlade – 'From the foothills of Black Mountain'

Stephen became involved in community, youth and environmental work through Newhill Youth and Community Centre. He later worked as a youth peer educator with the Upper Springfield Development Trust's Urban Initiative, before moving to Féile an Phobail as a community development worker between 2000 and 2003. He then worked as a youth development officer for Coiste na nIarchimí, before completing his degree in University of Ulster and taking up a post with Sinn Féin. Having spent his youth in West Belfast, Stephen later moved to Dublin, serving as Political Manager for Sinn Féin's team in Leinster House. He now works as an adviser to Sinn Féin's Northern Leader, Michelle O'Neill.

Steven's piece recalls his own early involvement with the Newhill Youth and Community Centre Féile float, right through to his role as Féile Events Manager.

Mark Thompson – *'A staple for our activism and our hope'*

Mark Thompson is a founder member and current Director of the regional victims and survivors' organisation, Relatives for Justice (RFJ). Mark has overseen RFJ's growth from a dedicated voluntary campaigning group to a professional human rights, advocacy and support organisation. Mark's experience in holding those responsible for human rights violations to account has included representing families at the United States Congress, the United Nations, European Parliament, European Court, as well as to governments in both Britain and Ireland.

Mark's piece details the central role that Féile has played in providing a platform to those seeking truth, justice, accountability, healing and recovery. It also recounts some of the truth campaign highlights over the years, such as the renowned Remembrance Quilt, the annual Plastic Bullet Vigil and the Ballymurphy Massacre Campaign.

Danny Morrison – *'Scribes'*

A lifelong republican activist and West Belfast native, Danny was twice imprisoned for his political activities, though recently exonerated and compensated, on the grounds of wrongful imprisonment, for his second spell in jail in the 1990s. A former Editor of *An Phoblacht/Republican News*, he later became National Director of Publicity for Sinn Féin. Upon his release, Danny became a full-time writer, and he has written numerous, critically acclaimed novels, plays and memoirs. He is secretary of the Bobby Sands Trust and was until 2014 the Chairperson of Féile an Phobail.

In his piece, Danny describes the foundation of the Féile's signature literary event, Scribes at the Rock, and recalls his own personal highlights.

Anne Cadwallader – *'The News Team'*

Originally from London, Anne Cadwallader is an experienced and well-known journalist. In the formative years of Féile's efforts to develop a radio station for West Belfast, she provided media training to Triple FM and later the Féile FM news teams. Anne has worked for the BBC, RTÉ, the *Irish Press*, Independent

Network News and Reuters, spending much of her career reporting on the north of Ireland. She is the author of *Holy Cross – The Untold Story* (Brehon Press, 2004) and *Lethal Allies* (Mercier Press, 2015), a ground-breaking investigation of state collusion with loyalists. In 2009, Anne left journalism to work for The Pat Finucane Centre for Human Rights in Armagh, as an investigator and case worker.

In her memoir, Anne recalls her experiences in providing Féile with news and media training as Féile Radio prepared to go live on air.

Phil Scraton – *'Féile: the personal is political'*

Phil Scraton is originally from Liverpool and began his 40-year career in research working with the Irish Traveller community. Now Professor of Criminology at Queen's University, Belfast (QUB), until 2004 he was Professor and Director of the Centre for Studies in Crime and Social Justice at Edge Hill University College. Phil is a well-known academic activist and has published widely on: the regulation and criminalisation of children and young people; controversial deaths and the state; the rights of the bereaved and survivors in the aftermath of disasters; violence and incarceration; the politics of truth and official inquiry; critical analysis and its application. In 2010 he was appointed by the British Home Secretary to the Hillsborough Independent Panel. He led the Panel's research, based at QUB, and was primary author of its report, published in September 2012. Phil was awarded the QUB Vice-Chancellor's Inaugural Prize for Research Impact in December 2012. His research has recently been shortlisted for another prestigious award – the *Times Higher Education* Research Project of the Year. Phil was also an advisor to the BAFTA award-winning documentary, *Hillsborough*.

Phil details his own experiences of Féile over many years coming as a visitor from Liverpool and then, when he moved to Belfast, through his involvement with Féile Radio and as a speaker at a range of events.

Pádraig Ó Muirigh – *'Providing our people with a life affording scope'*

Pádraig runs his own legal firm and specialises in a range of areas, including inquest law, legacy inquiries, actions against the police, human rights law, and judicial review. He is currently involved in high-profile campaigns relating to the Ballymurphy massacre, the Springhill massacre and Kelly's Bar bombing. Pádraig successfully applied to the Attorney-General to have inquests re-opened into the deaths of the 10 people shot dead by the British Army in Ballymurphy in 1971. He has also issued civil proceedings against the British Ministry of Defence and government on behalf of hundreds of former internees. Actively involved in the progressive development of law and the promotion of equality and social justice outside the courts, Pádraig supports the work of Inquest, a charity that provides legal expertise on state-related deaths, and is a member of the Inquest Lawyers Group and Haldane Society of Socialist Lawyers. He also sits on the Féile board and the Debates and Discussions Committee.

Pádraig's piece recalls his own Féile journey, from working on the festival security team to becoming a board member and member of the Debates and Discussions Committee. He explores some high-profile Féile events focusing on transitional justice and historical legacy.

Aislinn Higgins (Hagan) – *'Féile: something for everyone'*
Aislinn is a video journalist and radio presenter who cut her teeth as a teenage presenter on Triple FM and Féile Radio. After graduating with a degree in Media Studies from the University of Ulster, she worked for Below the Radar, the *Irish News* Online, Irish TV, and presented alongside Wendy Austin on BBC One NI's series 'In Your Corner'. Aislinn has recently launched her own boutique media production company, Dream Media TV, which provides video production and a range of others services. She remains active in Féile and continues to compere many of Féile's main events.

Aislinn's memoir recounts her early involvement in Féile and how it shaped her later media career.

Harry Connolly – *'Realising West Belfast's tourism potential'*
Born and raised in Ballymurphy, Harry spent many years as a youth worker and outdoor pursuits instructor with the Belfast city centre youth organisation, Challenge for Youth. Harry is the Director of West Belfast tourism agency Fáilte Feirste Thiar and has been instrumental in the development of the tourism sector in the area over the past ten years. In his current role, he is responsible for marketing Féile and attracting external sponsorship for the festival. He is a member of the Féile board and sits on its Debates and Discussions Committee. Harry is also an appointed member of the Fáilte Ireland Tourism board.

Harry's piece recalls his childhood memories of the local Springhill Festival and his later observation of Féile's growth and development. He concludes by focusing on Féile's tourism potential and outlines some of the major tourism capital projects currently earmarked for the west of the city.

Kevin Gamble – *'Minding the jersey'*
Kevin was born and raised in the Shaw's Road area of West Belfast and was educated through the medium of Irish at Bunscoil Phobal Feirste. With a back-ground in sports development, Kevin worked for the Brownlow Sports Trust, Craigavon, before taking up a post with the Upper Springfield Development

Trust in West Belfast as Community Sports Co-ordinator. Having joined the Féile board to promote sports development during the festival, Kevin eventually successfully applied for the vacant Director post in 2011. He has remained in the post ever since. During his tenure, Féile has undergone significant transition and growth.

Kevin's piece recalls his childhood memories of 1988 and the developing Féile before recounting how his own background in community sports development eventually led him to work for the festival. He considers his involvement in the most recent phase of growth and development for Féile before outlining his vision for continued development in the years ahead.

Introduction: Féile, culture and conflict in West Belfast

FEARGAL MAC IONNRACHTAIGH AND MICHAEL PIERSE

I'm no scholar. I've been a soldier, a sailor, a docker, a miner, on the seas and underground. I've seen much and made many a mistake, but despite all our flaws, I believe in my neighbour, my fellow man, my class. Meeting up and struggling to understand our lives as best we can. On our own, in isolation, we perish. The hall is a safe space where we can think, talk, learn, listen and laugh and dance. It's a good place. If I were a believer like you, I'd call it a holy place. It brings out the best in us. Don't be frightened. Come along, meet us. Talk to us, question us, but work with us. There is enough misery in the world already ... we are all one people, united in our beliefs with one common interest ... And not just to survive like a dog, but to live and to celebrate. (Yes!) And to dance, to sing, as free human beings (Loach, 2014).

So declares the socialist activist and visionary James Gralton (1886-1945), as depicted in Paul Laverty and Ken Loach's recent film, *Jimmy's Hall* (2014). Gralton's was a curious story, an uncomfortable reminder of the failures, and indeed fearfulness, of the post-revolutionary period dispensation. His controversial dance hall, the 'safe', even 'holy', space Gralton describes above, was the Pearse-Connolly Hall in Effrinagh, Co Leitrim. It provided access, in an increasingly theocratic, introspective and isolationist 1930s Free State, to culture in its myriad forms. For having the temerity to defy the Catholic Church, by giving poor people the chance to enjoy local and international culture — to study poetry, learn Irish, read books together, dance to jazz — Gralton was guilty of an affront then capable of being construed a crime. Unveiling a statue in Gralton's memory in Effrinagh, on 3 September 2016, President of Ireland Michael D. Higgins observed how Gralton 'created a place where his community could escape from the restrictions of a repressive social and cultural order that insisted on a narrow idealisation of our native culture being put under a conservative and clerical control that would culminate in the Dance Hall Act of 1934' (2016).

Gralton, declared an 'undesirable alien' in February 1933, was hounded by the church, government and right-wing elements of the IRA, and his hall was burnt down in an arson attack. Having went on the run from Irish men who had, barely more than a decade earlier, taken on the might of the British Empire in a briefly radical insurgency, he was eventually captured and in August 1933 shuffled onto a steamer in Cobh, Co. Cork, from whence he and his 'foreign' ideas would be safely banished to the United States. It was an extraordinary episode in a history of stifling conformity, during a period of aggressive anti-communism and reaction against popular culture in Ireland. The 'Gralton Affair' is a reminder of how apparently 'dangerous' (*read* liberating, enabling and exciting) unfettered access to culture can be for those hemmed in by forces determined that the 'cop in the head' — stifling intellectual creativity and curiosity — is just as effective as the cop in the streets.

The term 'cop in the head' often refers to techniques pioneered by radical Brazilian theatre practitioner Augusto Boal. These techniques helped people recognise how they had *internalised* oppression, a process relevant to both Gralton's 1930s hall and to those other 'undesirable aliens' who launched the West Belfast Festival in the late 1980s. At that time, the republican and nationalist community of West Belfast faced opposition to its cultural expression from a suspicious and hostile state. For some, the area had become synonymous with the *absence* of culture in its other definition — as the outcrop or guarantor of 'civilisation'. The narrative emanating from the established media often tarred the entire community with the same brush: 'men of violence' engaged in 'mindless' 'terrorism', as part of a 'savage', 'evil' and intractable conflict. The pen may be mightier than the sword, but this community received the sharp end of both. As Welsh Boalian theatre practitioner, Dan Baron Cohen, would quip in 1990s Derry: 'What use is the "Cop in the Head" when you have a cop in the front room?' (Grant, 1993: 10) His question here was surely partly rhetorical, however, given that his own sense that theatre could transform social and psychological relations in contexts of imperialist violence led to his work with Derry Frontline theatre group. This initiative undoubtedly challenged oppressive practices from without and within a community that felt itself under siege, much as Féile's own ventures into theatre would attempt to do.

Féile an Phobail's founders, like James Gralton flinging open the doors of the Pearse-Connolly Hall, sensed that access to cultural activities represented much more than light entertainment or fleeting relief from the terrible impact of armed conflict, though these effects cannot be ignored. As many of the following memoirs suggest, 'The Festival' represented something more fundamentally transformative: it brought the outside world in, allowed a community besieged by physical and representational violence to express its many talents and complex humanity — to rediscover its creativity and pride. It would help move West Belfast beyond the stereotypes, challenging the cop in the head and the cop in the street.

Like James Gralton, this community faced the prospect of being 'exiled', by the great and the good in the British and Irish establishments, as a people apart. For, as Bill Rolston's memoir notes below, 'government, media, academia and respectable society in general' were 'working off a mental map which in effect had written in huge letters over West Belfast: "Here be dragons". Féile, its founders thought, could both neutralise the havoc caused by annual Internment commemoration riots and produce a counter-narrative showcasing a compassionate, capable community of progressive, talented and determined people. Féile would, in the decades that followed, forge links with many currents in international arts and politics, and build bridges, too, with the unionist community. It would contribute to the unfolding peace process and open up uncomfortable conversations within its own community. It would, as Joby Fox argues below, empower 'real change-makers', who used their 'hall' to challenge, celebrate, laugh, reach out and debate.

On its 30th anniversary, while retaining much of its community-based ethos, Féile an Phobail now enjoys international recognition as one of Ireland's most iconic cultural offerings. Its journey is synonymous with the passage from conflict to peace in the north of Ireland and the memoirs below uncover insider perspectives on the fascinating story of how a community under siege responded positively and creatively during a period of brutalisation and marginalisation. *Féile Voices at 30* explores the challenges and triumphs of how a community expressed and transformed its culture through the cohesion and joy of a 'festival' in one of the most socio-economically deprived areas on these islands. The insights that follow are both an important part of Féile's celebration of and reflection on its journey over the past three decades and a resource for scholars, arts practitioners and community workers more broadly, in considering the role of 'festivalisation' in conflict resolution and community activism.

Originating from an Arts and Humanities Research Council funded research project at Queen's University Belfast, this memoir publication reflects the projects's initial goals of democratising research practices through a participatory methodology of co-creation, collaboration and partnership. As Luke Gibbons persuasively argues: 'understanding a community or a culture [...] means taking seriously *their* ways of structuring experience, their popular narratives, the distinctive manner in which they frame the social and political realities which affect their lives' (emphasis in original; 1996: 17). *Féile Voices at 30*, then, is informed by critical social research, which 'seeks out, records and champions the "view from below", ensuring the voices and experiences of those marginalized by institutionalised state practices are heard and represented' (Scraton, 2007: 10). These 'hidden voices' are often inaudible against the din of 'official histories' that propagate 'formally sanctioned knowledge', which upholds 'the determining contexts of material power relations' (ibid.). In prioritising these previously occluded narratives, this book aims to contribute to what John Pilger calls 'an insurrection of subjugated knowledge' (2006: 13). The following collection bears witness to the fact that 'politics and history are not made up of inconsequential and amorphous masses, and the experiences, values, opinions, and contributions of individual human beings count' (Buntman, 2003: 11). Crucially, this validates 'human agency' wherein 'social beings' interpret, evaluate and recount their real-life experiences of 'being there' during historical events (Scraton, 2007: 5).

'NÁ HABAIR É, DEAN É' – BUILDING COMMUNITIES FROM THE BOTTOM UP

As O'Leary and McGarry observe, 'the Irish euphemism for the conflict, "the Troubles", is just that: a euphemism' (O'Leary & McGarry, 1996: 18). Nearly half of the fatalities during what was a 30-year war took place in Belfast. Further-more, three quarters of these fatalities took place in the most socially-deprived North and West of the city (Sutton, 2001). Catholic civilians killed by security forces and loyalists, and security forces killed by republicans, constituted the two main groups killed during the conflict (McKittrick, Kelters, Feeney and Thornton, 2007: 1555). Added to this is the impact of disruption from militari-sation and imprisonment. It is difficult, therefore, to argue with the conclusion, made in Féile's first year, that while

> neither community in Northern Ireland has a monopoly of suffering in the present conflict [...] In relative terms it is undoubtedly the Catholics who have suffered the most, for it is against them that the main weight of repression has been directed. Most of the vast number of people impris-oned over the years for so-called 'terrorist' (i.e. political) offences have been Catholics and most of the victims of sectarian assassinations have also been Catholics (Rowthorn & Wayne 1988: 6-7).

West Belfast, therefore, bore much of the brunt of the conflict, from the late 1960s until the peace agreement in 1998 and beyond. While much of this mayhem resulted from policies hatched in Westminster and enacted, explic-itly or covertly, by state forces on the streets of Belfast, war also unleashed negative forces within the community, including the rioting that Féile sought to extinguish. Nevertheless, and as the testimonies below repeatedly remind us, resilience, good humour and humanity still shone through the darkest days.

Liz Curtis identified how republican violence 'dominates the coverage' of the conflict; she noted the tendency in the media of 'blaming the IRA' for violence regardless of the complexity of, or actors in, a given news item or situation (Curtis, 1998: 106–107). This bias corresponded with the implicit assumptions of British counter-insurgency strategy, wherein 'British and loyalist campaigns were symmetrical' and 'the loyalist paramilitaries' murderous war against the Catholic minority was regarded as reinforcing rather than undermining the security forces' war against the Provisional IRA' (Newsinger, 2002: 178). Media demonisation also served to polarise debate, limiting the space for constructive dialogue (see for example Miller, 1994). A community ostracised and ghettoised, 'The West' turned to various grassroots forms of political and cultural expression to make sense of its increasingly challenging political context and counter its misrepresentation. Local community activists frequently cite a *'ná habair é, dean é'* ('don't say it, do it') ethic that flourished in spite of, or perhaps because of, the 'Troubles'. This attitude fed a range of community responses aimed at bottom-up empowerment, not least in cultural terms. *Ná habair é, dean é* emerged from the local working-class Irish language activists who conceived, built and developed their own urban Gaeltacht against an unfavourable socio-economic backdrop and state hostility.

However, these very conditions, it is often observed, fostered a strong community cohesiveness and solidarity that emerged 'partly as a response to decades of economic and social disadvantage resulting from political discrimination and the suppression of cultural identity' (Leonard, 2004; see also, for example, McDonnell, 2008; Curtis 2014). The resultant activism inspired, for example, the Gaeltacht scheme whereby a number of young married couples, who raised and borrowed the money to purchase a piece of land on West Belfast's Shaw's Road, in 1969 eventually established Ireland's first urban Irish-speaking neighbourhood (Mac Ionnrachtaigh, 2013: 108). Although the planning and delivery of this initiative took nine years, the core group who spearheaded it 'never wavered in their determination to realize their goal' and succeeded 'without one penny of grant aid or government subvention' (ibid.). These events occurred against the backdrop of the Civil Rights movement, when the northern nationalist minority raised its voice against structural discrimination and socio-economic inequality. The new-found confidence of the late 1960s, manifested in marches demanding basic rights, mirrored the determined philosophy of these Gaeltacht activists.

With the onset of the conflict in the summer of 1969, these Shaw's Road activists rebuilt Bombay Street, off the Falls Road, which had been burnt to the ground by loyalist pogroms. Their practical skills and philosophy of self-reliance aided beleaguered nationalist residents under threat of Belfast Corporation-is-sued court proceedings, while the corporation refused to rebuild their homes, and under repeated violent attack from loyalists. This practical solidarity taught activists like Mac Seáin, 'nár leor streachailt Gaeltacht Bhóthar Seoighe ann féin agus gurbh éigeán dúinn dul i measc an phobail in am an ghátair. Rinne muid seo mar Ghaeilgeoirí, rud a d'ardaigh stádas na Gaeilge sa phobal' ('The struggle for the Shaw's Road Gaeltacht wasn't enough on its own and we needed to go amongst the community in its hour of need. We did this as Irish language activ-ists, which raised the status of the language in the community') (ibid: 109).

These same activists soon brought their model of self-help best practice to the Upper Springfield area of West Belfast, one of the most economically disadvantaged communities in the north of Ireland. They pioneered a series of community co-operatives to provide employment for local people, including Garáiste an Phobail (The People's Garage), Ballymurphy Enterprises and Whit-erock Industries. The professional architect on all these projects, Whiterock native Seán Magaoill, had also in the late 1960s designed the Shaw's Road Gaeltacht houses, along with Bombay Street and the Upper Springfield's first community hub, the Ballymurphy Tenants' Association. Describing his moti-vation, he stated:

> Ballymurphy was totally marginalised and excluded; it has massive social problems and was completely neglected by the council and the state. At this point, myself and Seamus Mac Seáin were working on Bally-murphy. We were completely focused on it. The only way we could help the community was to bring back some of their self-respect and show them that they could rebuild the place themselves (Dúchas Oral History Archive interview, from 10 February 2014).

These efforts, however, were hampered by the horrific circumstances of violent warfare that consumed the area at the time. Seamus Mac Seáin was shot five times by loyalists in November 1974 as he managed Garáiste an Phobail, while his co-worker, Geraldine Macklin, was killed (Mac Seáin, 2010).

Mac Seáin's survival would be crucial for future developments in West Belfast, as he would go on to play a leading role in ground-breaking projects such as the *Andersonstown News* newspaper, the West Belfast cultural centre, Cultúrlann McAdam Ó Fiaich, and the North's first Irish-medium secondary school, Meánscoil Feirste (now Coláiste Feirste). Magaoill's Whiterock Indus-tries facility, founded in 1971, would be destroyed by the British Army under the legal writ of emergency legislation. The army subsequently occupied the site for almost 25 years, constructing on it one of their largest military installations in the North, which would be known locally as Fort Jericho. When the British Army eventually vacated the site in 1999, Magaoill's long-term rent remuneration from the Ministry of Defence would be invested back into the burgeoning Irish-language community, whose growth would be synonymous with the growth and development of Féile itself. This is evidenced in the Irish-language memoirs below from Seán Ó Muireagáin and Jake Mac Siacais, and in the forthcoming BBC-commissioned documentary on the history of Féile an Phobail by Derry-based Irish-language film company Dearcán Media.

Paradoxically, these empowering cultural and community resistance practices were shaped by deeply traumatic experiences of death, imprisonment and oppression. The British Army was introduced to the North in August 1969, to support the RUC and ensure the survival of the unionist administration. In July 1970, it imposed a 36-hour curfew in the Falls Road area of Belfast to facilitate arms searches — a practice that would intensify significantly in 1971, when I carried out over 17,262 house searches (Lee, 1989: 433). When internment was introduced, on 9 August 1971, the majority of the 342 nationalists arrested from across the Six Counties had no involvement in the reorganised IRA. After a month, this number increased to more than 800 interned, the overwhelming majority of those drawn from the nationalist community. Over 2,357 people were arrested in the first months of Internment, with 1,600 being released after interrogation (Ibid: 439). In Ballymurphy, Internment was matched with three days of indiscriminate British Army shooting, from 9–11 August 1971, leading to the deaths of 11 local people, including the parish priest, in what would become known as the Ballymurphy Massacre.

According to Ballymurphy native Gerry Adams, 'with the effect of Internment [...] a community who had been either acquiescing, apathetic or essentially depoliticised had changed a 100 degrees' thus creating 'a popular uprising' and 'for the duration of what became known as the Ballymurphy riots, it was genuinely a battle a day' (interview with Feargal Mac Ionnrachtaigh, 30 May 2016). The British Army response was to intensify its efforts at imposing a military solution to quell the social unrest and the increasingly forceful IRA offensive. The efforts of this policy reached its apogee on Bloody Sunday in January 1972, when the British Parachute Regiment shot dead 14 civil rights protestors in Derry city. The international backlash essentially forced Ted Heath's government to suspend Stormont and impose direct rule, but two and a half years of British support for Unionist repression had wrought irrevocable damage and fuelled a working-class insurgency in West Belfast that would have appeared extremely unlikely in August 1969 (Farrell, 1976). This policy was manifested in Operation Motorman, in July 1972, which took place just days after a series of

IRA bomb attacks in central Belfast that became known as 'Bloody Friday' and claimed the lives of 9 people and injured another 130 (Lee, 1989: 442). Operation Motorman aimed at taking what were described as 'republican no-go areas' back under British Army and government control. Describing what occurred in Ballymurphy in this period, Ciarán De Baróid recalls:

> Operation Motorman happened in July 1972 and it was totally shocking [...] People rushed into Saracens [armoured British Army personnel carriers] and taken away to interrogation centres, people lined up against walls spread eagled; it was totally appalling. People being shot and killed under the slightest of pretence [...] Motorman totally battered the area and it was based on brigadier Frank Kitson's[1] counter insurgency ideologies and the idea was that you could destroy community interaction and that you would destroy the functioning of the community until everybody's sole purpose was self-preservation [...] It didn't work. People were incredibly resilient and they would turn the most horrendous experience [...] into a form of black humour and there is no weapon against that and guns don't work against that (interview with Mac Ionnrachtaigh, 23 February 2016).

It was against this horrific backdrop that the Upper Springfield Community Festival, a precursor to Féile an Phobail, was first envisioned, according to De Baróid, 'to lift people's spirits after Operation Motorman' (ibid.). It took place in August 1973 and without any recourse to statutory funding support. Organisers 'scraped a bit of sponsorship here and there', while 'the women of the area, quite spontaneously, started to make bunting — old clothes cut into little triangles and soon one street, then another street, then another street, until the whole area was festooned in bunting' (ibid.).

The festival's secretary, Noelle Ryan, outlined its aims in a letter appealing for sponsorship in July 1973:

1. To boost the morale and confidence of the community through community participation.
2. To encourage activities of a sporting, cultural and educational nature.

---

[1] One of the foremost British Army strategists in the North during this period, Brigadier Frank Kitson had previously served in British colonial conflicts in Kenya, Malaya and Cyprus, before being posted to Belfast in 1970. In his 1971 book, *Low intensity operations: subversion, insurgency, peace-keeping,* he wrote of making 'conditions [...] reasonably uncomfortable for the population as a whole [...] to act as a deterrent' (87).

3. To foster community development, community education and community relations in the greater Springfield area.
4. To sustain the festival as an annual event so as to develop a continuing sense of community awareness and to intensify community self-help.
5. To involve other areas in the future (original letter digitised in our Féile Online Archive).

These sentiments were echoed in the festival's programme, which was printed in its thousands and distributed throughout the area; in his foreword, local activist and priest Fr Des Wilson argued:

> A festival is a very happy event. At times, many of us thought we would never be able to celebrate again. We have had hard times indeed. But people share most in times of trouble and that is what our festival is about. [...] The festival was first thought of by a group of citizens who take different views on many things but agree on some very important issues. One is that in these days people need to become happy again — the festival is a morale boaster. Another is that people must work together for the good of the community — the festival is a co-operative effort. Another is that we need to think of the future — those who are together for this festival will stay together for much more to come. The Upper Springfield Festival is, we hope, a new beginning. In this spirit, it is offered to everyone who will celebrate with us (Féile Online Archive).

The festival was a resounding success, De Baróid recalls in his memoir below: it was 'one of the most participative events the district would ever see', where local 'people in their thousands spilled from their homes to pack the streets' and 'became part of the new unified social movement that eventually had more than 80 voluntary community groups looking after the needs of a single square mile.' Although the Upper Springfield Community Festival took place with similar success the following year, it also fell victim to the pressures of violent political conflict and hardship. However, undoubtedly it had planted a seed that would re-emerge again in the late 1980s under different circumstances.

Related and equally transformative community development practices would also emerge in the immediate aftermath of the Upper Springfield festival, under Wilson's leadership. Wilson, like many around him, would be increasingly radicalised and politicised by unfolding events during this period. His unequivocal and vocal support for the local community as the events of the 'Troubles' unfolded would inevitably lead him into conflict with both British military authorities and the catholic hierarchy. Wilson developed Springhill

Community House to promote cultural activity, community education and political empowerment. Influenced by the liberation theology then sweeping across radical and dissenting sections of the Catholic Church and embedded in neo-colonial conflicts in South America, he collaborated with local community workers and activists to encourage discussion and debate. Theatre and music were central to this programme, as were various fora for discussion, such as the 'Come n' Grumble' sessions organised in the mid-to-late 1970s. In these, a day would be set aside for a rolling debate on a diverse range of topical or controversial issues. Invited speakers would engage with transient audiences, who could come and go as they pleased.

Issues of local concern, from British counter-insurgency methods to criminal moneylending, healthcare, housing and unemployment, were also dealt with in plays, such as *The Soldiers Synge*, *The Merry-Go-Round*, *The Phone Call*, and *The Moneylender*. Writing of this bottom-up, self-help activism, Wilson argued that 'One way to understand what happened in the north of Ireland is to think of a constant creation of alternative education, alternative welfare, broadcasting, theological and political discussion, public inquiries and much else' (Wilson: 128). Diversion and comedy were also integral to these forms of grass-roots cultural activity, however. Living in a conflict zone produced a yearning for laughter and light relief, and variety shows, with music, magic, song, storytelling and comedy, drew on local talent, and in some cases local priests, who devised entertainments as a means of relieving tensions and providing short spells of escapist fun. This mixture, then, of political discussion, politicised art, and entertainment-as-release — a triad associated with the later Féile an Phobail — had much deeper roots in the fabric of West Belfast life.

THE 1981 HUNGER STRIKE AND ITS AFTERMATH

The British government's March 1976 decision to remove political status from republican prisoners would have profound and far-reaching consequences for communities like West Belfast. 'Ulsterisation, criminalisation, and normalisation' (Coogan 1980: 55) — central planks of Westminster policy toward the North — saw thousands arrested and interrogated under 'emergency terrorist legislation'. Many of those complained of torture and brutality (White, 2015), and it is estimated that as much as 80 per cent of convictions in this period were based on confessions extracted during intense interrogation (Hillyard, 1987).

At its essence, there was a core ideological function to this policy of criminalisation as a predominant justification for overtly political forms of containment. Criminalisation hinged on depoliticisation. It 'attempted to delegitimse the political motivation of anti-state activists and determined to create a moral distance between the state and other protagonists in the conflict' (Moen: 4). Criminalisation aimed to engineer popular support for repressive state action, calculating 'that people are more likely to support state action against a "criminal" act than they would the use of the law to repress a "political cause"' (Hall and Scraton 1981: 489). This new propaganda discourse adopted by the British government became pervasive in media and television representation during this period, whereby political prisoners became 'gangsters' and 'criminals'. But criminalisation of the IRA and republican prisoners extended more generally also, to the communities from which they came. Similar policies in another European context have been described as 'an essential element of a consciously waged psychological war of isolation and destruction' (Schubert, 1986: 189).

The community response to criminalisation in the prisons was to organise a mass campaign on behalf of prisoners, which developed organically from the mothers and wives of those imprisoned. They organised themselves into the what became known as Relatives' Action Committees (RACs), which later led to the formation of the National H-Block Committee. This dynamic movement would mobilise a national and international campaign against criminalisation, which developed as a broad-based, popular grass-roots movement that would both reshape and revitalise modern Irish republicanism for a generation (Ross, 2011). Nevertheless, despite significant national and international support for the prisoners' demand for political status, ten H-Block prisoners, three of whom were West Belfast natives, would subsequently die on hunger strike. The massive international reaction to the deaths of elected members of parliament on hunger strike severely embarrassed the British government, and resulted in the intense politicisation of nationalist/republican communities in the Six Counties (O'Hearn 2006: 376–78). Many of the memoirs below point to this period as key to understanding the dynamic behind Féile an Phobail.

The practical outworking of this intense politicisation and the impact of the grass-roots movement on community activism saw a shift in emphasis and widening perspective on how politics was defined. As Féilim Ó hAdhmaill recalls:

I remember in the late seventies going around collecting signatures for a survey in relation to Irish programmes on the radio and there were a couple of Sinn Féin leaders at the time who refused to sign it and said that the Irish language had nothing to do with the revolution because it was a remnant of old nationalism or Hibernianism and that only 'stuck up people spoke Irish' [...] before then, the movement only focused on the military campaign and there was a perception that the Irish language and even the prison campaigns were a waste of time as they were diversions from the war itself [...] the hunger strike changed this view and created a wider understanding of politics itself (Mac Ionnrachtaigh 2013: 159).

According to Aidan McAteer, a more strategic, political approach emanated from the 1981 hunger strikes. It broadened the potential for republicanism to effect political and social change from the bottom up:

> The struggle was a military struggle when I went into prison [in 1974]. By the time I came out it had spread way beyond that. I mean, electoralism hadn't kicked in. It kicked in with Bobby's [Sands's] election during his hunger strike. But certainly there was a clear movement towards community organisation, community politics. The language of course was enormously important and growing as something people wanted to revive and have as part of their identity and culture. All of that had taken off. I suppose even traditional music was much more central to the social life of nationalist-republican communities than it had been when I went into prison [...] community organisation was definitely part of the consequence of the hunger strike. Not to say that it started at that point, but certainly it was given an enormous boost. And the community structures that built up around the Relatives' Action Committees and the Anti-H Block Committees were at such a grassroots level that they then developed into community structures [...] people started to understand that they could organise themselves, in a way that I don't think they had before that (interview with Mac Ionnrachtaigh, 13 September 2015).

This point is echoed by Bill Rolston, an academic and Féile activist and contributor over many years, who argues that the aftermath of the hunger strikes created a space in which those who disagreed with aspects of the republican struggle, but who sympathised with it from a viewpoint of 'critical support', could 'say something and not be immediately in conflict with republicans' (interview with Mac Ionnrachtaigh, 23 January 2016). As Rolston argues:

> I regard the transformation as being the hunger strike, for me — not a republican prisoner, not a republican activist, an academic, community activist — and the hunger strike was a turning point because if you look at that most quoted quotation of Bobby Sands that appeared on the murals and everything else, 'that everyone has a part to play', that spoke to me because before that there were republicans who were telling me I had no part to play because I wasn't in the party or I wasn't in the army (ibid.).

For many, a spirit of outreach and collaboration had accompanied the newly developing political direction of the republican movement. Moreover, the post-hunger strike rise of republicanism as a political force saw British Prime Minister Margaret Thatcher and Irish Taoiseach Garret FitzGerald develop the 1985 Hillsborough Agreement in order to consolidate the constitutional nationalist position in the north of Ireland (McKeown et al, 1994).

For most, though, Sinn Féin was still a toxic brand, and it was clear too that West Belfast was fighting a very difficult battle over its representation, as evidenced recently, for example, in released state papers that convey the hostility of the Catholic hierarchy in the 1980s. In remarks made to an Irish government official in 1986, Catholic bishop, later cardinal, Cathal Daly commented on 'the working-class Catholic ghettos of west Belfast' where people are 'anti-establishment, anti-authority and anti-everything' (*Irish News*, 30 December 2017). A growing realisation dawned on West Belfast activists regarding the importance of this battle over representation, which might require a more flexible, creative and pro-active approach in challenging how the community was portrayed. Rethinking and developing alternatives to the damage done during the Internment commemorations would, however, require a major community-wide initiative.

DEALING WITH DEMONISATION: 'A NEW REFERENCE POINT FOR HELL'

'The warm welcome I receive here is even warmer during the Féile. There is no better all-round festival in the world.'
– Martin Sheen ('Féile Programme 2013': 6; Féile Online Archive)

'It is great to be here and participate in talent, in effort, in creativity, in genius in so many forms [...] This is truly a Féile an Phobail, to lift our hearts, to give us bright memories, shared memories, the kind of memories which build and renew communities.'
– Former President of Ireland, Mary McAleese (ibid.)

While the IRA developed a strategy of 'armalite and ballot box' in the early 1980s, through collusion and intelligence, the British had settled on a policy of containment; 'incapable of scoring an outright military victory, the notion of an "acceptable level of violence" developed, in which non-escalation of violence was deemed a relative success' (Tongue, 2002: 97). While the 1981 hunger strikes demonstrated that electoral support existed for the republican movement, the 1985 Anglo-Irish Agreement cemented a new British-Irish relationship and shored-up support for the SDLP, which clearly isolated republicans politically. Furthermore, the widespread negative public response to several IRA attacks, mostly notably the November 1987 Enniskillen bombing, fed this isolation, particularly south of the border. Nevertheless, the dominant state narrative of unreconstructed republican terrorism sat uneasily with the reality of a concerted military intelligence campaign of infiltration, an overt policy of shoot-to-kill against republican combatants and what is now widely recognised as systemic collusion with loyalist paramilitaries (see Cadwallader, 2013; Urwin 2016).

The events surrounding the funeral of three unarmed IRA members, Mairead Farrell, Seán Savage and Dan McCann, shot dead by the SAS in Gibraltar, in March 1988, brought the intensity of media condemnation to new levels. It also felt like a watershed for members of the West Belfast community; in his memoir below, Fergus Ó hÍr recalls:

> A vivid image of this period which stands out for me is of a sombre gathering late on a cold dismal night in March 1988 as people waited on Kennedy Way in Belfast for the bodies of three members of the local community, shot by the SAS in Gibraltar, to be brought back to their homes. As I observed the desolate scene, I remember the feeling that the situation in our community had reached a dark, depressing and dangerous low ebb.

When the 'Gibraltar Three's' bodies returned to Belfast, their funerals were attacked by loyalist Michael Stone, who shot and threw grenades at mourners, killing three of them. The shocking images were broadcast on screens worldwide, but more tragedy was to come. Days later, on 19 March, at the funeral of IRA member Caoimhín Mac Bradaigh (one of those killed at the previous funeral), a car drove into the cortege, then reversed at speed. Panicked mourners thought that once again they were under attack, some rushing to the car in an attempt to restrain its occupants. They broke windows and attacked the armed men, one of the occupants brandishing a gun, then firing a shot into the air, but soon having the weapon taken from him. The men, who were taken from the car and beaten by what was described across the media as a 'mob', were later discovered to be plain-clothed British soldiers Derek Wood and David Howes. They were shot dead shortly afterwards by the IRA, and a photograph of a well-known local priest, Fr Alex Reid, leaning over the dead bodies, which were stripped of clothes, became, as Tim Pat Coogan put it, 'one of the most searing images of the entire Troubles' (1996: 344). The mourning crowd became the subject of an outpouring of revulsion and condemnation. And this extended to a more general demonisation of republican West Belfast.

The Guardian commented on the attack under a very questionably worded headline: 'What happens when Irish crowds are angry: The collective rage behind Saturday's slayings'. Journalist David Hearst wrote:

> The catholic ghettoes of the Falls and Andersonstown Road are only a few hundred yards from the motorway that divides them from South Belfast, Northern Ireland and the rest of the world. But as they looked at themselves on the television screens on Saturday night, they could have been on a different planet, such was the gulf created by the last nightmarish days [...] nationalist west Belfast has always had the atmosphere of a city state. Many of its people never move out of their area, not even to shop in the town centre [...] Their lives are totally contained within these boundaries. It gives them everything except a job and a normal life. Only by understanding that cultural cohesion and desperation can one understand both the slaying outside St Agnes [sic] church on Saturday and the carnage in Milltown cemetery which preceded it earlier in the week. (*The Guardian*, 21 March 1988)

West Belfast apparently watched on in a collective 'silent, brutalised stare at a distant world, incomprehending and incomprehensible' (ibid.), as Hearst put it. Here was yet another brutal event that fed into a broader narrative. That narrative would claim to 'understand' *their* 'cultural cohesion' – the essentialised character of these othered 'Irish crowds' – which resulted in violence. Catholic Bishop Cathal Daly's public statement referred to 'evil forces that have been released within their community [...] evil that must be rejected totally and unequivocally' ('Hatred and "evil" of IRA denounced by bishop', *Catholic Herald*, 25 March 1988). Those responsible, he said, would 'not have taken iron bars into their hands to batter soldiers into unconsciousness if they had not first taken hatred into their hearts' (ibid.). The *Ulster Herald* commented that 'the devil himself had become manifest in the murderous mob responsible for this deed [...] the whole world could see what republicanism and violence has made of West Belfast – a paranoid community, dominated by masterplayers in the game of death' (*Ulster Herald*, 26 March 1988). Continuing in this vein, the editorial declared that 'the world could see [...] a community corrupted by violence'; 'to witness such violent savagery from people' had brought 'us very close to the state of political cannibalism'. Some years later, in a piece in *Fortnight* magazine entitled 'Images of a wild west', Paul Nolan considered the ways in which reductive and prejudicial representations of the West Belfast community proliferated in both TV drama and serious current affairs programmes: 'The fact is that television has found a new reference point for hell, and it is west Belfast' (*Fortnight*, issue 311, November 1992: 42).

The 'wild west' appeared to live up to its name, but these dark days fostered a determination among many to present a positive image of this much-maligned community. Hélène Hamayon-Alfaro writes, of the emergence of community arts in conflict-era West Belfast, that 'feeling that they were being misrepresented by the mainstream media — "demonized" was the term most commonly used — the Catholic community turned to the arts to produce a counter-discourse and assert its cultural identity' (2012: 47). In this analysis, a shrinking of the space in which this community could explain its position in the political sphere resulted in an efflorescence of self-expression in the cultural sphere. This turn to culture, although evident in the 1970s and 1980s, flourished in 1988.

At some level, Féile would seek to challenge well established patterns of generalisations about the Irish, particularly those from disadvantaged communities, which had been revived and applied to its community more particularly: the 'unsubdued Irish as being innately lazy, barbarous, bestial, amoral, bellicose etc.' (Mac Siomóin, 1994: 45). Anti-colonial theorist Albert Memmi would describe the representations in such negative stereotyping more generally in colonial contexts as 'mythical portraits' showing the oppressed as 'devious, treacherous, violent, over-fecund, irrational, emotional, inferior in education and skills, ungrateful, easily manipulated, superstitious, priest-dominated and in thrall to manipulative leaders' (Memmi 1998: 53-4). This rhetoric is used, according to Frantz Fanon (1961: 32), to justify the dehumanisation of colonial subjugation:

> As if to show the totalitarian character of colonial exploitation the settler paints the native as a sort of quintessence of evil. Native society is not simply described as a society lacking in values, but also the negation of values […] the enemy of values […] the absolute evil […] corrosive […] destroying […] disfiguring.

Such 'disfiguring' undoubtedly formed part of a pattern of rather questionable journalistic sociology when it came to the British-Irish conflict.

In recognition of the unprecedented levels of vitriol being directed at West Belfast, in August that year a small group of locals determined to counter the negative analysis of their 'cultural cohesion' (Hearst, above) by founding a festival that might celebrate their diversity instead. The logical turn towards cultural expression in the face of demonisation arguably overlaps with Fanon's radical decolonising methodology, whereby the elevation of cultural representation in order to reclaim and reframe a positive self-image forms part of a contrary construct to the colonial stereotype. For 'politically embattled minority movements', as Ella Shohat argues, such expressions enable a 'cultural self-definition, [which] however invented, is a crucial strategy for survival' (Carroll & King 2003: 9).

'TAKING THE BOOT OFF THE NECK OF THE PEOPLE' - FÉILE BEGINS

The idea of a West Belfast festival was originally initiated by the Sinn Féin MP for the area, Gerry Adams, who according to Deirdre McManus, 'got us together about the way West Belfast was being portrayed locally, nationally and internationally' to 'see how we could counter that and draw together some of the stuff that was already happening into a week-long festival' (interview with Mac Ionnrachtaigh, 31 January 2016). This aimed at 'taking the boot off the neck of the people' through 'trying to project an image of real West Belfast and to showcase all that was good about our community' (ibid.). Former Féile activist Danny Power, who would co-ordinate the festival in its early years, recalls how entertainment was always provided by makeshift local community and street festivals that were already a common occurrence. 'There were always smaller local festivals down in around Dunville Park,' he recalls.

> A lot of people will remember Pat McBride, who was of course later killed in 1992 in Sevastopol Street [...] Pat was a dedicated republican but also a bit of a madman who invested in disco equipment to organise discos for young people in the Lower Whack [the Lower Falls]. I was involved in this because Pat was in Sinn Féin at the time along with me. [...] He [Pat] bought the whole lot — decks, speakers etcetera. It was mad as hell [...] Pat's disco would be blasting out in the middle of rioting in the area and he revelled in the madness of it all (interview with Mac Ionnrachtaigh, 23 October 2015).

Although the annual Internment bonfires were becoming recognised, as Aidan McAteer points out, as 'a very destructive expression of our politics', whereby young people were 'injured [...] or being killed by plastic bullets', there had nevertheless 'developed discos, and maybe a bit of music around the bonfires' which was 'the core of what was later to develop as the festival' (interview with Mac Ionnrachtaigh, 13 September 2015). Therefore, as Jimmy McMullan's memoir recounts below, this first Féile committee aimed to 'give people a different focus for their energy — to turn it into something positive.'

The first Féile programme, which you can find fully scanned in our Féile Online Archive, included film screenings, snooker, handball, football and darts tournaments, a parade, a 'Lá Gaelach', folk concert, theatre, photo exhibition, 'Disco for the Disabled', fun day, fancy dress party and rock concert. It also incorporated lectures on historical themes: a '1930s Mill Workers' Day', a public debate on the twentieth anniversary of the Civil Rights movement, and a mural competition. The diversity of events, breadth of cultural forms, spirit of inclusivity and political emphasis evident here would remain mainstays of Féile for the next thirty years. But as Power recalls, 'it was pretty basic of course at this stage; the idea was to grab whatever resources you can get your hands on and only gradually it began to take shape into a programme of sorts to become a grander-scale festival' (interview with Mac Ionnrachtaigh, 23 October 2015). For Power, however, it had already achieved some fundamental aims:

> It was very well received because first and foremost we were organising fun activities and events for people to enjoy but primarily it was about the communities themselves. You know, getting a sense of their worth and not allowing themselves to be demonised as 'barbarians' (ibid).

Féile's capacity to organise 'from the ground up', most evident in the first two decades, as space for political mobilisation and expression opened up, would soon attract thousands of volunteers who worked in a range of capacities.

One of the most renowned and innovative expressions of this early energy was the development of the Springhill concert venue on derelict waste ground in West Belfast. McAteer describes the annual concert as 'a phenomenon' that was 'on the edge of legality, and that was part of the attraction of it, because it was such an act of rebellion' (interview with Mac Ionnrachtaigh, 13 September 2015). Community participation was central to Springhill's growth, as Tommy Holland's memoir in this volume points out:

> The Springhill Féile group consisted of Hector Heath's team, made up of local people, and our artist-in-residence, Gerard 'Mo Chara' Kelly, who all built the site and staging, and painted magnificent murals on them that would be just as good as any staging you would see at any major concert site.

Having first-time exposure to well-known music acts, such as Brush Shiels, Shane McGowan, Black 47 and Frances Black, had a huge impact on young people in the area, Seán Ó Muireagáin notes in his memoir below:

> Nuair a tháinig 'Springhill' ar an fhód, d'athraigh sé gach rud. Don chéad uair, bhí an t-aos óg in Iarthar Bhéal Feirste ag dul chuig gigeanna móra oscailte, rud nach ndearna ach fíorbheagán go dtí sin. Ba é seo an rud a thug léargas dúinn go dtiocfadh linne a leithéid a bheith againne fosta.
>
> (*When Springhill arrived on the scene, it changed everything. For the first time, young people from West Belfast were going to big open gigs, something that very few did at that time. This gave us the insight that we too could have access to such events.*)

Though these early festivals were supported through door-to-door fundraising, what emerged from very humble beginnings would become one of the most extensive and well-established festivals in the North's calendar of cultural events. But it would also dovetail with the community's efforts at capacity-building. As Fergus Ó hÍr articulates in his memoir:

> Like blossoming flowers, our neighbours, our friends and people whom we only knew as nodding acquaintances in the street, metamorphosed before our eyes into singers, writers, musicians, actors, organisers, artists, and sports stars, or revealed other talents which we had never imagined they possessed. West Belfast, so often vilified and excoriated by a biased, servile and self-serving media, stepped out during the week of the Féile and showcased a depth and wealth of talent and creativity that often surprised even ourselves.

Féile's role as a spur to community activism and cohesion is noted by activists right across its three decades in existence. Former Féile organiser, Chrissie Mhic Siacais, observes,

> From its earliest days, the bulk of hard work, organisation, the slog as well as the fun, joy and celebrations has been down to people on the ground. Local street and district groups are now better networked and co-ordinated but still retain the independence and freedom to fashion local events which really reflect local concerns, desires and not some manufactured image of what a 'festival' should be. It has been and will continue to be Féile's aim to encourage and empower the people of West Belfast, to provide a structured framework within which they can give expression to the creative talents and zest for life which are the hallmarks of this community. ('Féile Programme 1997'; Féile Online Archive)

Mhic Siacais's own work in community outreach focused in particular on the development of the carnival parade and associated street parties, which embedded the Féile throughout communities in the large, sprawling expanse of flat complexes and housing estates that stretch from the Lower Falls to Twinbrook and Poleglass. These street parties were organised by independent street committees, whose development was facilitated and supported by Féile. All 167 of them eventually became residents' groups — political organisation emerging from what began as grass-roots cultural and community activity.

One of the activists to work with Mhic Siacais in this period, who writes about the Springhill community festival in his memoir below, is Tommy

Holland. He refers to this political growth while giving credit to the inspiration and encouragement from Fr Des Wilson, who

> sent for us after the festival was over and said 'right, what are you going to do the rest of the year?' We said, 'work on next year's Féile'. 'What about setting up a Springhill Residents Association?' he replied. 'Look at the state of the houses and there's no play areas for the kids.' So, Fr Des got Joe Reid, who was a teacher and lecturer, to run a committee-management course for us in Springhill Community House. We later became a strong residents' and lobbyist group, and we never looked back. The old Springhill estate was demolished and the houses built to a high standard and a beautiful children's play park is now on the derelict site that the festival was on.

The festival would host a range of diversity initiatives right from the beginning. Talks and events on anti-racism, disabilities, gender equality, and, in later years, LGBTQ rights, have been frequent in Féile programmes, and as Claire Hackett's piece below for instance attests, some of these initiatives were aimed at challenging the West Belfast community as well as challenging perceptions of it from the outside. The initiative Hackett writes of, 'Irish, Queer and Equal?' (2000), 'set a very strong context of discussing LGBT oppression within other forms of social justice struggle — class, race and gender equality', which was ultimately about 'building alliances and linking struggles'. Travellers and disability advocates would form part of the festival parade and other events from the 1990s; a 'Celebration of Traveller Culture' mural, for example, would be unveiled at Féile in 1995. Events highlighting disability issues also recur throughout the three decades. This overall emphasis was noted by English barrister Michael Mansfield, who would comment on the 'vibrancy and diversity' of the festival and its 'contribution towards building a community with different horizons [...] There should be many more such projects throughout the inner city areas of the UK' ('Féile Programme 2013'; Féile Online Archive).

'A WHIRLWIND OF IDEAS' - EXPRESSING, EMPOWERING AND EXPANDING THROUGH FÉILE

Part of Féile's success, then, was its capacity to platform an impressively diverse range of activities, catering to a broad range of social, political and cultural interests, which attracted many who were initially oblivious or even hostile to the festival. Former Féile Director Deirdre McManus describes this phenomenon as 'a whirlwind of ideas [...] where there was an amazing energy and creativity and where anything and everything was on the table: so long as you made it work, then it could happen; there was no barriers' (interview with Feargal Mac Ionnrachtaigh, 31 January 2016). Many familiar with Féile will comment on the extraordinary multiplicity of its activities, from international discos to traditional music competitions, dance workshops, arts groups, 'An Céilí Mór', historical tours of West Belfast, exhibitions, plays, major musical acts, conservation activities and sports competitions. The range of miscellaneous activities over three decades includes the infamous guider races, tug of wars, bonny-baby competitions, water balloon fights, wheelie-bin races, helicopter tours, bog oak art, the 'Saracen Jeep' experience, samba soccer summer schools, skateboarding classes, computer-game battles, pigeon races, freestyle dance, charity boxing matches, fishing trips, talent shows, street pantomime, day-trips for disadvantaged youths, painting classes, and orienteering.

In his memoir, Terry Goldsmith describes his and others' environmental campaigning, reminding us how

> environmental conservation was very low on most peoples' agendas in those days and we were very pleasantly surprised by the genuine interest shown in our project. You have to remember that back in the mid-1980s 'saving biodiversity' still meant putting your whites in with your dark wash.

Goldsmith describes how outdoor events developed and became integral to the festival. Raising awareness on conservation and providing enjoyable outdoor recreation would be matched by a campaigning and advocacy drive that would lead to the The Bog Meadows 'being designated an official local nature reserve'. This dynamic was also evident in the late Terry Enright's[2] annual Black mountain walk, which became a staple of Féile. As Eilish Rooney writes, in her memoir:

> [Enright would] bring us over to the great hole being gouged out of the side of the mountain by the quarry corporation. We'd stand, not too close, looking into the pit. Terry would talk, urging us to activism, and take off again, us in his wake. The craic was ninety and the day endless. A place that was once our Ballymurphy playground became, thanks to Terry, an education in resistance and a story of love for people and place.

Similar to the Bog Meadows campaign, these excursions would have an awareness-raising capacity, playing a part in the environmental community activism

---

[2] Enright is the father of *Féile Voices at 30* co-editor Feargal Mac Ionnrachtaigh.

that would culminate in the National Trust purchasing Divis mountain and a section of Black mountain in 2005, thus realising, as Goldsmith states, 'the dreams of our late friend, Terry Enright, by acquiring and opening up' the mountains for community access.

Féile's hosting and promotion of historical walks and tours had a similarly transformative impact, as described by Tom Hartley in his memoir. He recollects how the historical bus tours he led in the early Féile gradually developed into walking tours of the City and Milltown cemeteries, and how the research he conducted for these tours led to two books about the complex and often contradictory histories of those buried there. Hartley's work in this regard thus enriched his sense of the interconnectedness and nuance behind the political divisions in northern Irish society, something that informed a programme of political outreach to unionism that he embarked on behalf of Féile. As Jim Gibney recalls:

> It struck Tom that Féile could provide a platform for unionists to speak to the nationalist and republican people of West Belfast and vice versa. And so began an engagement between unionists, nationalists and republicans, in halls and on stages across West Belfast, at the height of the summer season in the midst of war, with all its human consequences. Out of these fledgling beginnings began a discourse between republicans and unionists that would develop in intensity and make a valuable and significant contribution to the IRA calling its ceasefire in August 1994.

This relationship with the developing peace process was vital to Féile's progress from the very beginning. The process commenced in secret through the Hume-Adams talks, which took place during the early years of the festival, but only began to raise public hopes for a peace accord as momentum built in 1990s.

Féile would play an important role in attracting key speakers and breaking new ground with historic debates at packed and often heated events each August. Many of these discussions marked key milestones and historic shifts of position as the process developed. The Féile committee was instrumental in attracting then Irish President Mary Robinson to the area in June 1993. Her public engagement with Gerry Adams on that occasion — when the issue of public figures meeting the Sinn Féin leader was still a political hot potato — was widely read as symbolising the Republic's desire to reach out to and include northern republicans in the coming political process. This was followed later when Albert Reynolds, on the invite of Gerry Adams, officially opened the new Féile an Phobail offices, Teach na Féile on the Falls Road, on 25 March 1997.

Féile's potential to grab the headlines through high-level political outreach was again illustrated in June 2018, when Taoiseach Leo Varadkar agreed to launch the Féile 30' programme amid controversy. The Fine Gael leader was forced to 'defend' his association with Féile (Ní Aodha, 2018) amid criticisms from unionism — which seemed odd given the attendance of DUP members at previous Féile events. Féile's willingness to break new ground and challenge people both within and without the West Belfast community is described by Pádraig Ó Muirigh in his piece below:

> The D&D group has carried on that Féile tradition of being brave and bold. One of our mottos is that Féile 'does firsts'. In recent years, I have introduced Martin McGuiness and the PSNI Chief Constable, George Hamilton, to speak at Féile. I also helped organise an event where Orange Order leader Mervyn Gibson shared a platform with my father, Sean Murray, a former IRA prisoner.

Similarly, McAteer argues that:

> One of the great strengths of the festival is its ability to reach out and be inclusive [...] It's one of the few places that it happens, that political opponents are invited in and listened to with respect. All that plays into the development of the peace process and politics, and the festival is part of that (interview with Mac Ionnrachtaigh, 13 September 2015)

A range of renowned thinkers, writers and activists from across the local sectarian divide and internationally, have continued to speak at Féile events, which created space for constructive political transition. By opening this space, Féile has, according to Phil Scraton's piece below, 'generated and consolidated inclusivity across communities beyond West Belfast's boundaries.'

If many of the discussion and debate events have been 'outward-looking', reaching across barriers built over the long conflict, many have also been about the republican community answering back. A persistent feature of Féile has been its use as a public platform for many outstanding truth and justice campaigns such as those concerning the Ballymurphy and Springhill massacres, or the banning of plastic bullets. Féile organisers argue that these debates have allowed republicans a 'fair hearing' unavailable in other fora. In this sense, Féile has helped facilitate the growth of activist groups and community organisations, as affirmed below by Mark Thompson, who spearheaded the development of Relatives for Justice (RFJ) from its origins as a voluntary victims' group to its current role as a rights advocacy nongovernmental organisation. In bringing the families of the Ballymurphy and Springhill massacres together for the first time in Féile 1999, under the rallying call 'no hierarchy of victimhood', RFJ helped those families organise a fresh truth and justice campaign. As Thompson recalls, in this book, of the role of Féile:

> Féile has always provided an important platform in which marginalised voices are heard and valued, where new creative, imaginative and challenging ideas are encouraged, discussed and debated. Where activism happens. Where we try to be solution-focused. And this type of activism and these qualities are central to RFJ, so Féile was and remains a staple for our activism and our hope.

Many of the memoirs below attest similarly to the role Féile played in the life of West Belfast.

Among the most significant engagements with the arts through Féile has been its fostering of theatre. The late director Pam Brighton, herself a major driver of Féile's theatrical output in the 1990s and 2000s, wrote of how the festival had

> a history of bringing what is interesting, new and innovative in the professional arts to West Belfast, both during the festival and throughout the year. This combines with the artists' collective, JustUs, Roddy's and Conway Mill Writers' Groups to generate an explosion of talent that is singular to Féile ('Féile Programme 1997'; Féile Online Archive).

An important part of the festival, which even in its most basic and cash-strapped form in 1988 featured a documentary play by Ulick O'Connor, *Execution*, has been its capacity to bring theatre to West Belfast and bring West Belfast to the theatre. Dubbeljoint Theatre Company, founded in 1991 by Brighton, Marie Jones and Mark Lambert, premiered Jones's localised adaptation of Nikolai Gogol's *The Government Inspector* in 1993, along with Terry Eagleton's *The White, the Gold and the Gangrene* that same year. But the troupe's role extended well beyond the conventional ambit of commercial theatre; it acted also as a spur to grassroots involvement. During Féile events from the mid-1990s, Brighton and her team for instance conducted workshops aimed at encouraging budding theatre directors and producers.

Her guidance helped Chrissie Mhic Siacais and a group of local women with no background in professional theatre to establish JustUs Community Theatre in 1995. While their co-production of the following year, *Just a Prisoner's Wife*, premiered in the spring and thus outside of the festival, it had emerged from a

Féile initiative. Mhic Siacais, Féile's then community development worker, had originally brought the JustUs group together to organise an event pertaining to local women's lives to commemorate International Women's Day. The group would go on to produce major theatre productions, including *Binlids* (written by Jake Mac Siacais, Danny Morrison, Brenda Murphy and Christine Poland; 1997) which travelled to New York in 1998 under the spotlight of the international media. They also produced the somewhat controversial *Forced Upon Us* (written by Brenda Murphy and Christine Poland; 1999). Mhic Siacais and Poland were both products of the Falls Women's Centre nucleus that was established in 1982 'for women, by women', as Úna Ní Mhearáin observed, as a 'safe space for women amidst so much poverty, hardship and trauma' (NVTV, *Falls Women's Centre*). Both theatre groups were responsible for guiding people previously untrained in theatre into later careers in the profession.

And if this theatre gave the community an opportunity to tell its story from the perspective of West Belfast natives, it also created space for these young women to be reflective and self-critical: watching *Just a Prisoner's Wife*'s all-female cast playing men and presenting women's (sometimes critical) attitudes to aspects of the republican struggle, one is struck by the extent to which JustUs was challenging patriarchal norms in West Belfast, even as much of its criticism is directed at the British state. In her memoir, summarising the impact of these experiences, Christine Poland writes:

> Community theatre has many benefits, and as individuals we gained them by the boatload. It builds self-confidence, stimulates imagination, creates empathy, and encourages cooperation and communication skills; it aids concentration and also stimulates fun. Additionally, it's an emotional outlet; it enables the hurt and oppressed to express themselves without censorship. It's a powerful tool for conflict resolution; and it grows an appreciation for arts and culture. JustUs gave leadership to other groups — 'if we can do it so can you', we'd proclaim. So the company went on to raise its own issues using drama.

The central productive force behind Dubbeljoint and one of the inspirations behind JustUs, the Bradford-born Brighton had emerged from her experiences in left-wing theatre in England. Her theatrical nous was honed at the Royal Court theatre and as far afield as Canada, though Brighton had a long-term affiliation with community theatre in Belfast. She was joined by others — such as Tom Magill, John Goodchild and Bill McDonnell — who, having also gained extensive experience on the left-wing English theatre scene, would bring those experiences to theatre in West Belfast. Magill would, as Mícheál Mac Giolla

Ghunna recounts in his piece for this book, provide 'the invaluable guidance and support' in facilitating H-Block republican prisoners as they adapted Bobby Sands's poems for the stage. Inspired by Augusto Boal's 'Theatre of the Oppressed', these prisoners would be invited by Féile to showcase their resultant play, *The Crime of Castlereagh*, at the festival in 1996, and Mac Giolla Ghunna and company would be released on parole from the H-Blocks and driven directly to St Agnes's Hall in Andersonstown for a 'bizarre and bewildering experience to be, after breakfast in the Blocks, suddenly back in the outside world' where 'we performed our work that night to over 500 people and to a rapturous reception'.

Féile was equally instrumental to the staging of Irish-language plays through Aisteoirí Aon Drama and later the professional Irish-language theatre organisation, Aisling Ghéar. It also opened itself up to perspectives (including those of loyalist writers) that were opposed to republicanism. The festival has equally supported looser forms of theatre, ranging from variety to vaudeville to satirical revues, such as those by the Ad-Hoc Theatre Group. Plays and films have continually been produced on campaigns and community work-centred topics. Féile's wide-ranging theatre output contains a multiplicity of themes and aims, from the personal to the political, the serious to the frivolous, the artistically complex to the politically transparent. The festival provided a variety of fare to suit diverse tastes, though always the tendency is toward the political.

The continuing success of the festival's theatrical outputs is illustrated by the emergence of further local theatre, such that staged by Brassneck Theatre Company, which was established in 2007 to develop 'new writing from its firm West Belfast roots addressing themes of identity, history, culture and religious and racial tolerance' (Brassneck, 'About Us'). Notably, even now its organisational objective echoes the mission of the early Féile: 'the re-imaging of West Belfast, endeavouring to break the pre-conceptions that exist about this part of our city' (ibid.). Company Director Tony Devlin has written, acted and produced plays such as *1981* (2011) and *Belfast Rising* (2016), while also directing plays such as *Man on the Moon* (2014) and *Holy, holy bus* (2014). At the time of writing, to coincide with the 30th anniversary of the festival, Féile has commissioned Devlin to write and produce a play on the history of festival.

Non-commercial community radio was another aspect of Féile that could trace its origins to the 1970s. Féile FM first broadcast in in the late eighties as an illegal pirate radio station operating from the Springhill area of West Belfast. But it followed much earlier, illegal ventures in local radio in Belfast — Radio Free Belfast (broadcasting from 1969-1970) and pirate Irish-language radio station Raidió Fáilte, which has been in intermittent existence since 1984. In July 1996, Féile decided to relaunch Féile FM as Triple FM, under a one-month license. The radio station, which broadcast across the city in spring and summer, one month per season, provided opportunities for young people to learn broadcasting basics through hands-on experience and an Open College Network training course in radio skills and management. Some of these volunteers progressed into media careers, having been originally mentored by the journalist Anne Cadwallader, who outlines her involvement with the station in this memoir collection. In her memoir, Veronica Brown describes her experiences of working as station manager:

> With each broadcast we became more professional and updated our equipment. The quality of our advertisements improved greatly and this aided us in generating sponsorship for individual programmes. All money made contributed to the running of the station and paid for the licences. We never received funding, so we relied heavily on this money. I remember we didn't even have paper for writing requests, so we called on the local community groups to donate scrap paper that could be used for this purpose […] Over the 28 days of broadcasting, we had over 200 volunteers involved.

Gerard Hodgins, who worked at the station in this period, lauded how West Belfast 'buzzed to the anarchic, offbeat, downbeat and anybeat sound of raw festival radio as brought to you the great unwashed by the great unwashed' ('Féile Programme 1997': 5; Féile Online Archive). In 2001, the station was rebranded Féile FM and opened its own premises, though it moved to and from various locations over the years. While communications regulator Ofcom granted the station a full community radio license in 2005, with full-time broadcasting commencing in 2007, its inability to establish long-term financial sustainability caused the station's closure in 2011. However, Stephen McGlade argues in his memoir that, in a context of censorship, this '24/7 news and entertainment service' played an important role in the West Belfast community. It was, he reminds us, 'before the internet or Sky TV and also during the period of broadcast censorship banning Sinn Féin from the airwaves, so this way you got to hear the politics and real news.' As well as delivering a sympathetic media outlet for the West Belfast community, Féile FM allowed Féile to promote itself when positive media exposure was more difficult to come by.

In a number of contexts, Féile's ambition as the festival expanded provided a boost for the arts across Belfast. It also demystified and rendered accessible artistic practices and realms from which working-class people often feel alienated (see Bennett et al., 2009; O'Brien and Oakley, 2015; Belfiore et al., 2016), especially in terms of theatre, but also with regard to film. In explaining his motivation for establishing the West Belfast Film festival in 1995, Laurence McKeown remembers observing that film was 'the only thing missing at that time from the Féile programme' because 'the medium of film and filmmaking was still largely regarded at that time as the preserve of the elite or privileged, something outside the reach of working-class communities' (McKeown's memoir, below). McKeown got permission from radical film-maker Ken Loach to show a 'sneak preview' of Loach's *Land and Freedom* during the first West Belfast Film Festival. Film-industry celebrities such as Martin Sheen, Tom Berenger, Stephen Fry and Stephen Rea would subsequently visit the film festival, thus garnering significant publicity for Féile. In 1997, the festival received a modest funding boost that enabled it to change its scheduling to September and extend its programme on a city-wide basis. It was eventually renamed the Belfast Film Festival, under the stewardship of long-time Director, Michele Devlin. Féile has continued to screen films and collaborate with the Film Festival, including in outdoor venues. McKeown remains an active member of its board and is also a member of the board of management of Northern Ireland Screen, which has the 'collective goal', he writes, of establishing 'a purpose-built film centre in Belfast, similar to the Irish Film Centre in Dublin' (ibid.).

Its capacity to attract household names has also been a notable feature of Féile's signature literary event, 'Scribes at the Rock'. Established by Danny Morrison in 2001, with the support of then Féile Director Carol Moore, 'Scribes' aimed to 'lure into West Belfast some major writers to do readings, but in an intimate setting, without airs and graces' (his memoir, below). Local creative writing groups were given the opportunity to read alongside renowned 'writers, poets, screenplay writers, theatre directors and actors'. Summarising the impact of 'Scribes', Morrison writes:

> Although a small event, it attracts the most prestigious of writers on the Irish literary scene and beyond. And, while local people have the opportunity to hear at first hand major writers read from their work, those writers themselves experience a little bit of the hospitality, warmth and friendliness of West Belfast and go away as ambassadors for a once-beleaguered, now incredibly proud and confident community.

In the memoirs collected here, Féile activists repeatedly cite their commitment to challenge long-standing notions of and barriers to cultural participation, and its inclusivity and accessibility for working-class communities has arguably distinguished Féile from many festivals on these islands.

FÉILE AT 30 AND BEYOND

By the 2000s, Féile was on a firmer footing financially, its foundation of a separate series of springtime events, titled Féile an Earraigh, in 2004, signalling confidence in the festival's ability to continue to expand into new areas. Féile's central involvement into the late 1990s in spearheading the vexed campaign for a St Patrick's Day festival in Belfast's city centre entailed a fractious but ultimately fruitful battle with Belfast City Council for recognition and funding. This and its own struggles in previous years have perhaps left the festival well placed to compete for funding and ticket revenue in the post-Crash climate of austerity that has caused arts funding to be repeatedly slashed in the North over recent years.

However, like all grass-roots community organisations or social movements that receive a (welcome) increase over time in statutory funding (Ó Croidheáin 2006: 315), Féile has grappled with concerns regarding its potential institutionalisation, assimilation or manipulation by the state. Ethical and ideological tensions, between bottom-up, grass-roots imperatives — which often prioritise community ownership and counter-hegemonic resistance — and the inevitable requirements for increased development, sustainability, professionalisation and commercialisation that statutory funding entails, arguably become more complex and multi-layered in post-conflict situations. Lisa Slater notes for example, in an Australian context, how

> indigenous festivals […] have grown in tandem with state policies that foster the celebration of culture as a further means to govern people. For all the positive aspects [… these festivals] operate within a web of government and non-governmental agencies and corporate agendas and power relations. Indeed, funding and supporting such events could be regarded, in some instances, as cunning forms of governmentality (2014: 140).

In the north of Ireland, for example, the reality of widespread 'social injustice and material deprivation' as 'determining, structural contexts' has challenged the official discourse of a successful 'society in transition' (McAlister, Scraton and Hayton, 2009: 156). Furthermore, the trans-generational trauma of the conflict has left a legacy of marginalised, disadvantaged and under-resourced communities whose collective alienation seems most prevalent amongst the young (ibid). The practical consequences of this alienation are referred to by McAteer who, speaking of Féile, argues: 'we're not involved in a life-and-death struggle any more, but we were then' while 'there's a lot more division and a lot less cohesion in the community since then' (interview with Mac Ionnrachtaigh, 13 September 2015).

Féile has thus also undergone intense internal debate about its future direction and sustainability, which has often been defined by demands for renewal, expansion and change. This dynamic is apparent in current Féile Director Kevin Gamble's memoir below, where he writes of starting his post with Féile in 2011 with the view that the festival had 'somewhat lost its edge — lost its connection to, or appeal for the local community'. Gamble argues that 'a whole new generation of young people were growing up with no real connection or appetite to engage with the festival programme'; he recalls that he 'set about developing a new vision for the "relaunching" of Féile, locally, nationally and internationally, transforming the entertainment element of the festival, moving it to a bigger stage, attracting more top artists and bringing in even bigger audiences'. This departure required a significant increase in resources; as Harry Connolly states in his memoir, developing 'new relationships with statutory tourism and marketing bodies' and intensive lobbying 'to ensure that we got our fair share' became key activities in this regard. A visit to Milwaukee Irish Fest, to promote Féile 25' in 2013, inspired Gamble, he notes, with the 'dream to develop the Falls Park into a Féile HQ festival site'. As Connolly recounts:

> With the health and safety regulations well and truly in place, we nevertheless transformed our own green lung, the Falls Park, into a new event space, in the spirit of Springhill. Over the past five years this new venue has attracted a host of top music acts, catering for all genres and all tastes. Féile has succeeded in bringing world-class acts to local people at Féile value; some of these acts have sold out various venues in Ireland for more than double the price of a Féile ticket. This is the power and true spirit of Féile. I'm sure that those who were in the 'Big Tent' in the park and felt the atmosphere when UB40 blasted out 'Red, Red Wine', or when we chanted with the Kaiser Chiefs' 'I Predict a Riot', were reminded, like I was, that this is what Féile is about: amazing summer nights spent in an electric environment with proud West Belfast people (Connolly's memoir, this volume).

Yet the extent to which the festival has leveraged its opportunities to expand and cater to new and bigger audiences — or indeed, the extent to which this is desirable without compromising its radical political focus — is a debate that will continue to define the future direction of Féile and any academic scholarship that seeks to evaluate its importance. Aidan McAteer's contention that Féile 'needs to stand on its own integrity and not compromise its core values and its core politics in order to become part of the mainstream' gives expression to this challenge (interview with Mac Ionnrachtaigh, 13 September 2015).

In post-colonial contexts, grassroots expressions of community life like Féile an Phobail can encapsulate 'a powerful transformation of trauma into a celebration of resilience' (Rooney, 2000: 222) and a 'bottom-up embodiment of community empowerment and recognition' (Bean, 2007: 101). Participatory forms of cultural expression have enabled historically marginalised communities to translate their counter-hegemony for wider audiences and thus attain social and cultural capital of their own. As the memoirs below demonstrate, the West Belfast community's ambitious and ground-breaking engagement with arts practice through Féile produced social and economic empowerment, physical and urban regeneration, cultural exchange and conflict resolution in a context of acute political violence and significant political transition. Further research on the festival will no doubt enhance our understanding of the complexities, tensions, disagreements and inconsistencies inherent in the Féile project (some of which are referenced or suggested in the memoirs), but our research thus far has demonstrated the undoubted significance of this festival, both in the local context of a society transitioning from conflict, and in a wider context of debates on 'cultural value' (see Crossick and Kaszynska, 2016), participatory arts, and 'festivalisation' (see Bennett, Taylor and Woodward, 2016).

Our current Féile research project, funded by the Arts and Humanities Research Council, will publish more scholarship on this festival in coming years, as we sift through the sixty or so interviews that we have conducted with former Féile activists and staff, along with the memorabilia, ephemera and documentation that our crowd-sourcing project has unearthed in partnership with the local community. Funded under the AHRC's 'Translating Cultures' programme, the Féile History/Stair na Féile project emerged from a collaboration between Margaret Topping and one of the current authors, Michael Pierse, at Queen's University Belfast. The other editor of this collection, West Belfast native Feargal Mac Ionnrachtaigh, came on board thereafter as a researcher and has expanded the project's ambition.

From the beginning, the research team prioritised building a working partnership with the Féile staff, board members and its wider community, in order to garner trust in the research team and foster co-creation and collective ownership of the project. In addition to this memoir publication, we are expanding our physical Féile History exhibition with a series of short videos to be launched at Féile 30; we have supported Derry-based Irish-language film company Dearcán Media with research advice for its forthcoming BBC-commissioned documentary on the history of Féile; we have provided Tony Devlin and Brassneck Productions with archival support for his forthcoming play on the history of Féile, *A Station Once Again*, which is also being launched at Féile 30; and we have also developed a partnership with West Belfast-based oral history archive, Dúchas, to store and make available to the public our collection of interviews. We hope that this process will help facilitate the Féile community as it reflects

I

critically on both the enduring legacy of the festival and on challenges in terms of its future direction.

This book of memoirs provides an opportunity for prominent Féile activists to express what the festival has meant to them. Such a process is necessarily imperfect, uneven and contradictory: memories are not always accurate; at times, events can be conflated or confused; and as we have found, many former Féile activists disagree — sometimes fundamentally — on the current trajectory of the festival. Equally, the collection below reflects the views of activists who have engaged with our project, but we are conscious that other views remain to be recorded and we welcome further contributions to our growing oral history archive. Our intention here has been to let a range of opinions and recollections speak as they are, and we are grateful to those who have contributed to the volume and shared what are often powerful, inspiring, insightful, thought-provoking, funny, or indeed difficult, memories of their experiences. What emerges is a rich tapestry of opinion and recollection which, we hope, enhances our understanding of what Féile has meant for West Belfast, and what its lessons can mean for festivals, cultural practitioners and community activists worldwide, not least those emerging from conflict.

WORKS CITED

Aiken, Nevin T., *Identity, Reconciliation and Transitional Justice: Overcoming Intractability in Divided Societies* (New York: Routledge, 2013).

Bean, Kevin, *The New Politics of Sinn Féin* (Liverpool: Liverpool University Press, 2007).

Belfiore, Eleonora, Jonothan Needlands, Catriona Firth, Natalie Hart, Liese Perrin, Susan Brock, Dominic Holdaway, and Jane Woddis, *Enriching Britain: Culture, Creativity and Growth* (Coventry: University of Warwick, 2015).

Bennett, A., I. Woodward, and J. Taylor (eds.), *The Festivalization of Culture* (Aldershot: Ashgate Publishing, 2014).

Bennett, Tony, Mike Savage, Elizabeth Silva, Alan Warde, Modesto Gayo-Cal, and David Wright, *Culture, Class, Distinction* (London: Routledge, 2009).

Beresford, Tom, *Ten Men Dead: The Story of the 1981 Irish Hunger Strike* (London: Grafton, 1987).

Brassneck, "About Us" [accessed online, 17 July 2018] https://www.brassnecktheatrecompany.com/about.

Buntman, Fran Lisa, *Robben Island and Prisoner Resistance to Apartheid* (Cambridge: Cambridge University Press, 2003).

CAIN – Conflict and Politics in Northern Ireland online archive, http://cain.ulst.ac.uk/sutton/.

Cadwallader, Anne, *Lethal Allies - British Collusion in Ireland* (Dublin: Mercier, 2013).

Carroll, Claire and Patricia King (eds.), *Ireland and Postcolonial Theory* (Cork: Cork UP, 2003).

Carroll, W. K, "Hegemony, counter-hegemony, anti-hegemony", *Social Studies* 2 (2006), 9–43.

Clayton, Pamela, "Religion, Ethnicity and Colonialism as Explanations of the Northern Ireland Conflict," in D. Miller, ed. Rethinking Northern Ireland (London: Longman, 1998), 40–54.

Cleary, Joe, "'Misplaced Ideas?' Colonialism, Location, and Dislocation in Irish Studies," in Claire Carroll and Patricia King (eds.), *Ireland and Postcolonial Theory* (Cork: Cork UP, 2003), pp. 16–46.

Coogan, Tim Pat, *On the Blanket: The H-Block Story* (Dublin: Ward River Press, 1980).

---. *The Troubles: Ireland's Ordeal 1966-1996 and the Search for Peace* (London: Arrow, 1996).

Crossick, Geoffrey and Patrycja Kaszynska, *Understanding the Value of Arts & Culture: The AHRC Cultural Value Project* (Swindon: Arts and Humanities Research Council, 2016).

Curtis, Jennifer, *Human Rights as War by Other Means: Peace Politics in Northern Ireland* (Pennsylvania: University of Pennsylvania Press, 2014).

Curtis, Liz, *Ireland: The Propaganda War* (London, 1998).

Devine, Adrian, and Frances Devine and Clare Carruthers, "Developing a Community Festival Admidst Civil Unrest", in Allan Jepson and Alan Clarke (eds.), *Managing and Developing Communities, Festivals and Events* (Basingstoke: Palgrave, 2016), pp. 165–178.

Fanon, Frantz, *The Wretched of the Earth* (London: Harmondsworth, 1961).

Farrell, Michael, *The Orange State* (London: Pluto, 1976).

Féile Online Archive, www.feilebelfasthistory.com.

Gibbons, Luke, *Transformations in Irish Culture* (Cork: Cork University Press, 1996).

Grant, David, *Playing the Wild Card: A Survey of Community Drama and Smaller-scale Theatre from a Community Relations Perspective* (Belfast: Community Relations Council, 1993).

Hall, S. & P. Scraton. "Law, class and control" in M. Fitzgerald, G. McLennan and J. Pawson (eds.), *Crime and Society: Readings in History and Theory* (London, 1981), pp. 460–79.

Hamayon-Alfaro, Hélène, "Empowerment through the Arts: Community Arts in Belfast in the 1980s and 1990s", in Cécile Coquet-Mokoko and Trevor Harris (eds.), *Crafting Identities, Mapping Nationalities* (Newcastle upon Tyne: Cambridge Scholars, 2012), pp. 41–56.

Higgins, Michael D., "Speech at the unveiling of a monument to Jimmy Gralton" (2016) [accessed online, 16 July 2018] www.president.ie/en/media-library/speeches/speech-at-the-unveiling-of-a-monument-to-jimmy-gralton.

Hillyard, Paddy, "The Normalisation of Special Powers: from Northern Ireland to Britain", in P. Scraton (ed.), *Law, Order and the Authoritarian State* (Milton Keynes: Open University Press, 1987), pp. 279–312.

Hughes, James, "Frank Kitson in Northern Ireland and the 'British way' of counterinsurgency", in *History Ireland* 1:22 (January/February 2014) [accessed online, 7 June

2018] www.historyireland.com/volume-22/frank-kitson-northern-ireland-british-way-counterinsurgency/.

Kitson, Frank, *Low intensity operations: subversion, insurgency, peace-keeping* (London: Faber and Faber, 1971).

Lee, Joseph, *Ireland 1912-1985: Politics and Society* (Cambridge: Cambridge University Press, 1989).

Leonard, Madelene, "Bonding and Bridging Social Capital: Reflections from Belfast", *Sociology* 38:5 (2004), 927–944.

Loach, Ken (Director), *Jimmy's Hall* (Sixteen Films: 2014).

Mac Ionnrachtaigh, Feargal, *Language, Resistance and Revival- Republican Prisoners and the Irish Language in the North of Ireland* (London: Pluto Press, 2013).

Mac Seáin, Séamus, *D'imigh sin agus tháinig seo – Scéal oibrí fir i mBéal Feiste a linne* (BÁC: Coiscéim, 2010).

Mac Síomóin, Tomás, "The Colonised Mind – Irish Language and Society", in Daltún Ó Ceallaigh (ed.), *Reconsiderations of Irish History and Culture* (Dublin: Léirmheas, 1994), pp. 42–71.

McAlister, Siobhán, Phil Scraton and Deena Haydon, *Childhood in Transition - Experiencing Marginalisation and Conflict in Northern Ireland* (Belfast: Save the Children, 2009).

McDonnell, Bill, *Theatres of the Troubles: theatre, resistance and liberation in Ireland* (Exeter: University of Exeter Press, 2008).

McKittrick, David, Seamus Kelters, Brian Feeney , Chris Thornton and David McVea, *Lost Lives: The stories of the men, women and children who died as a result of the Northern Ireland troubles* (Edinburgh: Mainstream, 2007).

Memmi, Albert, *The Colonizer and the Colonized* (New York: Orion Press, 1965).

McKeown, Laurence, Brian Campbell and Felim O'Hagan (eds.) *Nor Meekly Serve My Time: The H-Block Struggle 1976–81* (Belfast: Beyond the Pale, 1994).

Miller, David, *Don't Mention the War: Northern Ireland, propaganda and the media* (London: Pluto Press, 1994).

Moen, Declan, "Irish Political Prisoners and Post Hunger-Strike Resistance to Criminalisation", in George Mair and Roger Tarling (eds.), *The British Criminology Conference: Selected Proceedings. Volume 3: Papers from the British Society of Criminology Conference, Liverpool, July 1999* (British Society of Criminology, 2002).

Newsinger, John, *British Counterinsurgency: From Palestine to Northern Ireland*, (Basingstoke: Palgrave & McMillen 2002).

Ní Aodha, Gráinne, "Varadkar defends launching Belfast festival: 'Olly Murs is headlining – he's hardly a die hard republican'" [accessed online, 17 July 2018]: http://www.thejournal.ie/leo-varadkar-feile-an-phobail-olly-murs-4057676-Jun2018/.

Ní Mhearáin, Úna, *Falls Women's Centre*. TV programme [accessed online, 18 July 2018] http://archive.northernvisions.org/specialcollections/ogfeatures/falls-womens-centre/.

Nolan, Paul, "Images of a Wild West", *Fortnight* 311 (November, 1992), 42.

O'Brien, David, and Kate Oakley, *Cultural Value and Inequality: A Critical Literature Review* (Swindon: Arts and Humanities Research Council, 2015).

Ó Croidheáin, Caoimhghín, *Language from Below: The Irish language, Ideology and Power in 20th Century Ireland* (Bern: Peter Lang, 2006).

O'Hearn, Denis, *Nothing but an Unfinished Song: Bobby Sands, the Irish Hunger Striker who Ignited a Generation* (New York: Nation Books, 2006).

O'Leary, Breandan and McGarry, John, *The Politics of Antagonism: Understanding Northern Ireland* (London, 1996).

Phoenix, Éamon, "State papers: Cahal Daly warned Catholics are 'anti-everything'", *The Irish News* (30 December 2016) [accessed online, 10 July 2018] http://www. irishnews.com/news/2016/12/30/news/working-class-catholics-anti-everything-said-cahal-daly-855975/.

Pilger, John, *Freedom Next Time* (London: Bantam, 2006).

Richards, Anthony, "Terrorist groups and their political fronts", in James Dingley (ed), *Combating Terrorism in Northern Ireland* (London: Routledge, 2008), pp. 54–77.

Rooney- Rooney, Eilish, "Learning to Remember and Remembering to Forget: Beloved from Belfast", in Lynn Pearce (ed.), *Feminist Readings in Home and Belonging* (Aldershot, 2000), pp. 215–34.

Ross, Stuart, *Smashing H Block: The Popular Campaign against Criminalization and the Irish Hunger Strikes 1976-1982* (Liverpool: Liverpool University Press, 2011).

Rowthorn, Rob and Wayne, Naomi, *Northern Ireland: the Political Economy of Conflict*, (Cambridge: Polity Press, 1988).

Scraton, Phil, *Power, Conflict and Criminalisation* (New York: Routledge, 2007).

Schubert, Michael, "Political Prisoners in West Germany: Their situation and some consequences concerning their rights in respect of the treatment of political prisoners in international law", in Bill Rolston and Mike Tomlinson (eds.), *The Expansion of the European Prison Systems, Working Papers in European Criminology 7* (Belfast, 1986), pp. 184–194.

Slater, Lisa, "Sovereign Bodies: Australian Indigenous Cultural Festivals and Flourishing Lifeworlds", in Andy Bennett, Jodie Taylor, and Ian Woodward (eds.), *The Festivalization of Culture* (Burlington, VT, Ashgate: 2014), pp. 131–46.

Sutton, Malcolm, "An Index of Deaths from the Conflict in Ireland" [accessed online, 18 July 2018] http://cain.ulst.ac.uk/sutton/.

Tongue, Jonathan, *Northern Ireland: Conflict and Change* (Edinburgh: Pearson Education Limited, 2002).

Urwin, Margaret. *A State of Denial: The British Government and Loyalist Paramilitaries* (Dublin: Mercier, 2016).

White, Lisa, *Transitional Justice and Legacies of State Violence – Talking about torture in Northern Ireland* (London: Routledge, 2015).

Wilson, Des, *The Way I See It* (Belfast: Beyond the Pale, 2005).

From little acorns:
the Upper Springfield Community Festival

CIARÁN DE BARÓID

Memory can be fickle, but the idea of a community festival, as far as I can recall, was first floated to me by Frank Cahill in May of 1973. Frank, who lived in Ballymurphy and had been central to many of its community development initiatives since the early 1960s, felt that the festival would give people a lift after the terrible state brutality that had been Operation Motorman. What became the Upper Springfield Community Festival was, I believe, the inspiration for Féile an Phobail.

Initially, the idea was to have been a Ballymurphy festival; but in line with efforts of the time to cement the eight housing estates of Ballymurphy, Spring-hill, Whiterock, Westrock, New Barnsley, Moyard, Dermott Hill and Springfield Park into some form of coordinated community development project, it was decided to extend the festival to include all eight estates. In an effort to bridge some of the then bitter political divisions within republican areas, all shades of opinion agreed to participate in the organisation and operation of the festival.

In those days there were no grants for events like this. Yet, the idea immediately captured the imagination of everyone across the eight housing estates. The dates were set for August 12th to 19th 1973 and a magnificent organisational feat got underway. Every community group and facility in the area became energised. Events were planned centrally by the festival committee and they were planned by everyone else at the local level – down to the very streets. Even Fred Bass's annual summer play scheme was absorbed into the whole. A huge billboard, it was decided, would be erected above the Ballymurphy 'Bullring' shops. Using a pegboard and large moveable letters, the events of each day could then be advertised for all to see. (Admittedly, there were a few unexpected messages up there some mornings, but generally, the board was spared abuse.) Money was raised locally and from a small number of outside sponsors, and prizes were bought. And, without any prompting, the women began to make bunting from

1

old clothes, first one street, then another, until the whole area was festooned in an ocean of fluttering colour. Then the organising committee faced the question of military activity.

'We can't have children playing in the streets and bullets flying everywhere,' 18-year-old Kate McManus said. 'There needs to be a ceasefire.'

'Is everyone in agreement with that?' Charlie Heath from Westrock asked. Charlie was Chair of the committee.

'Agreed,' Jenny Quigley from Glenalina Park said and everyone nodded.

'Well, that's simple,' Steve Pittam laughed. 'Charlie can get both sides by the scruff of the neck and just bang their heads together.' Steve, a Quaker volunteer based in Moyard, had been one of those who had brought Fr. Hugh Mullan's body off the street after he'd been shot dead by British paratroopers during Internment Week in 1971.

'The IRA won't be a problem,' Frank Cahill said. 'We can talk to some people about the place here and they'll sort that end out. That just leaves the Brits.' We all agreed that 'just' was a great word. But Frank continued, undaunted. 'We need to send someone up to the Taggart to talk to the Major.'

'I wonder who we could send?' Charlie Heath asked.

'You!' Frank said without hesitation. 'The best person to send is always the Chair.'

Whether that was true or not, we all agreed, and Charlie was dispatched off to the Taggart the very next day. An hour later he came back. 'That place is very bad for the bangers,' he declared. 'I'm never going back near it again.' 'What happened?' he was asked. 'Well, whenever I arrived, they wouldn't open the gate. Then, in the end, when they let me in, I was brought into the Major's office at gunpoint. "NAME!" the Major bawls as soon as I walk through the door. "My name is Charlie Heath," I tell him. "I'm here to see if there could be a wee ceasefire during our festival…" "ADDRESS!" your man bawls and that's how the whole thing goes – him bawling his head off and me trying to explain all about the ceasefire … I don't think it went very well.'

But, in the end, we got the ceasefire, unspoken but effective, with no hostilities from either side from August 12th to 19th 1973. Sometimes humanity broke through the crust of war like that.

On August 12th the festival got under way with a big parade. Well, it wasn't really a big parade. The Liam McParland Accordion Band (two of whose members had been wounded by loyalists firing from Springmartin the previous May) came marching up the Whiterock Road, followed by a couple of hundred people. Frank Cahill's wife, Tess, and Jan McCarthy, whose partner Pat died in Ballymurphy during Internment week, were there. Gerry Finnegan, the previously Methuselah-bearded local community development officer was there, stripped to the waist and white as a ghost, with his great beard shorn away. Steve Pittam was there with a small crowd from Moyard, carrying banners, flags and a couple of whistles and balloons. It didn't look like much, but it was the beginning of one of the most participative events the district would ever see. Since then, there have been many festivals; but apart from Upper Springfield mark two, the level of community participation has never, in my opinion, been equalled or surpassed.

There were no great props and there was no fancy equipment. People clapped their hands or blew a whistle to start the sack race. At the other end, two people held a piece of string. To accommodate the kids' parties, families brought chairs and tables from their homes, made cakes and biscuits, and sealed off the streets with bins so the kids could have them to themselves. In the clubs there were old-time waltzes and discos and pensioners' nights and bingo. There were guider races and tugs-of-war and fancy-dress. The street theatre put on by Fred Bass's play scheme was led through the district by a painted clown in a bowler hat. In the women's netball tournament, Big Alice Franklin of Ballymurphy turned out a scary team dressed in white shirts, knee-length woollen socks and short, red pleated skirts, who beat the crap out of all opposition to take the coveted cup. At the Bonny Babies competition, the judges fled once their decision had been made. There were music nights and debates and painting competitions and 16-milimetre movies, including the historical classic, *Mise Éire*. And some enterprising young people cracked open the fire hydrants in several streets to provide fountains in which overheating kids could dance. Unfortunately, there lingers no great photographic record; but the photos that do exist show a community determined to give it the best, while the massive notice board announced the offerings as the days progressed. And while people in their thousands spilled from their homes to pack the streets, they also became part of the new unified social movement that eventually had more than eighty voluntary community groups looking after the needs of a single square mile. And they kindled the idea of a West Belfast festival which was attempted in 1975 but didn't have the organisational spread needed to make it the big success that had been hoped for. However, from little acorns grow mighty oaks …

Féile an Phobail would come in its wake.

From humble beginnings

Jimmy McMullan

I started working with the festival committee when it was set up in 1988. We felt there was a need to try and reflect the spirit and resilience of the people in Belfast and the West in particular. Traditionally, the period around the 9th of August was marked by an anti-internment demonstration, which usually ended up in days of rioting due to attacks on the march by British forces.

We felt that having a festival in this time period would give people a different focus for their energy — to turn it into something positive. The first festival committee was born, made up of individuals and community activists. At our first meeting, we discussed the budget — a discussion which lasted all of two minutes as we had absolutely no money. Events were planned regardless of how we intended to fund them (there would be a lot of arm twisting). Special mention must go to the immense goodwill of local people who provided us with their skills and resources free of charge. People on the committee were given various roles, i.e. from funding, organising and liaison with local areas, to publicity and formulating strategy. I found myself in the role of concert organiser. I was joined in this task by Hector McNeill, Brendan Hughes, Tony Carlisle and Jim Moody to name just a few. Others would come on board at a later date.

We decided that we needed a name for our group of concert organisers and adopted the grand title of 'Hot August Night Productions'. We felt we needed to attract artists from far and wide if we were to break down the negative image presented by the communities' enemies. So where to start? One of the group got us an introduction to a major promoter and we went to meet him to present our case. We asked him for help. He was supportive, but couldn't commit time to the project. He did, however, persuade Sinéad O'Connor's manager to meet with us. A time was arranged and our group headed to Dublin for the meeting, which took place in Jurys Hotel. O'Connor's manager was Fachtna Ó Ceallaigh. He listened to what we had to say about our reasons for starting the festival. He thought for a while and said, 'I'll do everything I can to help you succeed.'

He told us that he couldn't commit Sinéad to perform at our first festival but that we could meet her in person and present our case. We ended up in Sinéad's hotel bedroom and I could tell right away that some of our group were completely star-struck (Jim Moody).

She told us that she wouldn't commit to performing but that she would visit during the festival to see for herself the work we were doing and if the mood was right she would do an ad hoc performance. As it turned out the visit was cancelled due to a development with a certain 'Prince'. Fachtna in turn was true to his word and would go on to open many doors for us in the years to follow. We talked with him about setting up a pirate radio station (he was based in London at the time) and before we knew it he had sent the equipment to broadcast along with an 'engineer' called 'Lexsy'. We were greatly impressed with his professionalism until he donned a pair of washing up gloves and said, 'I'm not leaving my fingerprints on this shit'. I thought Hector was going to explode with laughter. Our early attempts at 'broadcasting' were farcical, but we did lay the ground for the community station eventually emerging and getting a license to operate in later years.

Our first year's concerts were to take place in the Andersonstown Leisure Centre and we decided in our wisdom to hold them outside on the football pitch. We were joined by a brave band of volunteers (no not that kind!) led by John O'Carroll, who sent about building a stage, which was a health and safety nightmare. Our line-up was completed and the day was to be kicked off by a local hero Rab McCullough and his band Baraka joined by Micky Lawless and O'Carrolls RIP. We had about ten local bands who were performing for free. The headline act was to be Energy Orchard led by Joby Fox and the late Bap Kennedy. They were based in London at the time and just secured a record deal. They agreed to come home if we paid their travel expenses. Brush Shiels and Band were also booked to play. We had to negotiate a fee (which made us really nervous because we had no dough). We were to be totally reliant on door takings to pay fees.

As it turned out, the rain caught us out and we were forced to move to a ramshackle marquee set up outside the Andytown Social Club. The gang that 'erected' this marquee had laid it on waste ground and the inside walls were covered in muck (I thought I was back in the Blocks!). There was no floor covering on the inside and the ground was covered in holes and high puddles of water as the rain hammered down outside. It looked as if we were finished before we started. The old saying 'if you build it they will come' turned out to be true. People were up for a party come what may and we ended up with a packed marquee and Brush Shiels belting out 'Dirty Old Town'. The Century Steel band also played that night (all the way from Coventry) and when Bap and Energy

Orchard sang 'Sailor Town' they brought the house down, literally, when part of the marquee collapsed. It looked like disaster had finally struck, until a bunch of people came running in with what looked suspiciously like a telegraph pole and propped the roof back up again to the roar of approval from the crowd. That night turned out to be one of many to remember. We even made a bit of money. Brush Shiels sent us back his fee for the evening with a message that he would do all he could to support us. A true gent.

I think it's important to remember that Féile grew out of very humble beginnings, brought forward by people with little financial resources but plenty of voluntary effort. The British government had been attempting to isolate West Belfast, referring to us as a 'criminal community' and starving the area of any economic or community stimulus. We were met with opposition from officialdom and access to local amenities closed off. When we decided to move our opening day parade to the Falls Park due to the growth of the festival, we were locked out by Belfast City Council. Mysteriously, the locks fell of the gates by the time the parade reached the park and the rest, as they say, is history. The festival was and is of course much wider than the few concerts we put on. Local areas were organising themselves with their own activities and productions, none better than the legendary Springhill Festival, led my Gerry 'Mo Chara' Kelly and his merry band of followers, but that's a story on its own I suspect.

In memory of Seán Lavery

Aidan McAteer

Standing (or swaying to be more accurate) in the Féile marquee last August, it was hard to absorb the enormity of change in circumstances, in atmosphere, in attitude and in mood from that first Féile back in 1988. The sense of enjoyment and fun was the same but in every other way things are so, so different.

The first Féile took place in a very dark time. The context was war, division, repression, resistance, defiance. At that time the conflict was all-pervasive and immediate. West Belfast was the most militarised and most heavily patrolled area in Europe and probably, at that time, in the world. Loyalist killings, harassment, arrests and imprisonment were part of the daily life of an entire community. People hung on every news bulletin, in a cycle of violence with West Belfast as a regular feature, and not always as the victims — as resistance, passive and active, was also a part of the daily life of the community.

But in the midst of the conflict swirling around us, life did go on and normal human activity in all its rich diversity flourished. Despite the effects of the cycle of violence that caused such deep pain and suffering at individual and family levels, there was never any sense of paralysis, or despair, or resignation at a collective community level. Paradoxically, the everyday challenges of life in West Belfast through the so-called 'Troubles' may have actually heightened the appreciation of life and living, of friendships and enjoyment. The Féile, I believe, both reflected and tapped into this mood.

Rich creative talent exists in every community in the world, but is rarely recognised or provided for by those who define culture and art in narrow, elitist terms. In West Belfast, so unjustly vilified and starved of resources by the state, this creative talent was also crying out for a platform. And the sense of unity of the West Belfast community, under attack physically, politically, economically and culturally, probably brought a sharper, more political edge to much of the talent and creativity of the area, motivated by a defiance that may not have existed in a less challenging environment.

7

West Belfast was, and still is, a highly educated, politicised, culturally aware and creative community. The disgraceful characterisation of the community as 'savages' and 'terrorists' was entirely inaccurate. In fact, the opposite was the case. And after the terrible events of Gibraltar and its aftermath there was a palpable demand that the bigoted, politically driven stereotyping of our community should be challenged and confronted. And there were also many people outside of our area who were appalled by the derogatory labelling of a whole community as less than human. Anyone who had taken the time to study, even at the most cursory level, the history of Ireland, of the six-county state, of the civil rights movement and of the Troubles, quickly saw through the lazy and politically driven prejudice of blaming the victims of injustice and repression for a conflict not of their making.

Members of the Irish diaspora and many politically progressive activists from across the world, including artists, actors, writers, musicians and others, understood that there was a deeper, more complex story than the tabloid headlines portrayed, but they had little opportunity to express their solidarity with the people of West Belfast and beyond. So, in the summer of 1988, all the ingredients were already in place: a vibrant and highly motivated community, acutely aware of its history, culture and identity; talent that had never been recognised or appreciated by the formal arts sector; and internationally recognised artists who wanted to offer their help and support. Féile an Phobail was waiting to happen; it just needed a catalyst. And in early 1988, Gerry Adams took the initiative and convened a meeting of local community activists, writers, artists and musicians. From that point forward, planning for the first ever West Belfast Community Festival began in earnest.

When the festival took off, the enthusiasm and energy was immediately infectious, with spontaneous street parties and mini-fleadhanna in almost every street. Féile grew year on year, drawing in bigger names to perform alongside emerging local talent. But alongside the festival, the darkness continued.

For me, the stark contrast between the fun and joy of the Féile and the pain and suffering that so often visited our community was most tragically felt on 8 August 1993. That day, a nationalist march had for the first time reached Belfast city centre — from which we had always been excluded. There was an enormous feeling and roar of celebration as the march turned towards City Hall, and our spirits were lifted by the success of our campaign to break the ban. Just hours after we made our way back from the city centre, a loyalist death squad, armed and directed by British intelligence, opened fire on the home of Sinn Féin councillor Bobby Lavery and killed his young son, Seán, in a savage act of revenge.

We immediately considered cancelling all events on that closing night of the festival, but quickly decided that this would hand a victory to the murderers and their controllers. Instead, the concert in Springhill that night was louder and went on later than normal, with music blasting out across Belfast into the early hours of the morning. I sincerely hope that the killers and their British Army handlers heard the music that night and realised that while they could inflict deep hurt at a personal and family level, the community they had attacked remained defiant, unbowed and unbroken.

And, of course, the name says it all: Féile *an Phobail*. It was from the start the people's festival, organised by the people and building from street level. Despite the communal punishment of political vetting and censorship that denied West Belfast the funding available to other communities, the people of this community created — through their own resources and rich talent — the most successful community festival in Europe.

Go n-éirí leis agus linne.

Bród

DEIRDRE MCMANUS

In 1988, in the aftermath of the killings of IRA volunteers Mairead Farrell, Seán Savage and Danny McCann in Gibraltar, the attack on the nationalist community intensified and focused on West Belfast. This constituency had been at the geographical heart of the conflict in the north of Ireland from the late 1960s. In an effort to counter this, Gerry Adams (MP and President of Sinn Féin) gathered a crowd of us to pull together what became the West Belfast Community Festival.

West Belfast was demonised by the Brits and their supporters as the 'terrorist community'. Their strategy was to demonise and put us down, while the community strategy/response was to have fun, enjoy ourselves, fling the doors open wide, engage, and embrace. We would be in charge of our own image — locally, nationally, and internationally. We would showcase all that was good about West Belfast. We were proud of what we had to say … and lucky to do this by way of a FESTIVAL! Imagine, the 'enemy' strategy was to demonise, while the community strategy/response was to have a festival.

The festival would do many things, but first and foremost it would give the people of West Belfast a well-earned party and a chance to celebrate. We would showcase all that was good about us. In essence, this meant we would oversee the co-ordination and organisation of a number of things: an Opening Day Carnival Parade, a festival programme, a film festival, publicity, concerts, debates, drama, exhibitions, sports, funding, sponsorship and administration. It might sound like we did everything, but that isn't the case: we broke it all down into smaller groups, which were, as such, autonomous and naturally formed i.e. people signed up to work on one, two, three or all of the above, or came up with their own ideas. Groups on the ground would continue to do their own thing. Groups that had their own focus were encouraged to join us, be involved. When the festival started, we were pushing at open doors within our own community; people were glad to see us coming — everyone wanted to be part of it.

Bród: *Deirdre McManus*

Danny Power was the first coordinator in 1988 and I was lucky to come in behind him and pick up on the work that he had already started. Eventually, we got an office, in the very early 1990s, in An Chultúrlann. It was about the size of a box room and became the central hub. At that time, those intensely involved and who made it happen were Siobhán O'Hanlon, Tony Carlisle, Angela McEvoy, Danny Power, Gerry Adams, Aidan McAteer, Geraldine McAteer and myself. We had many balls (and balloons) up in the air at any one time, and we weren't too sure at times how things would pan out. But everyone was on board, and even though the work was hard, it was great to be a part of it.

We agreed that the festival would start on the first Sunday in August and continue for the following week. We went into action: talked to groups and individuals and got them to commit; gathered information about activities; set deadlines; printed a programme and made it happen. We shared information, especially on anything to do with resources and funding, which was in very short supply. Our amazing, positive community groups had been starved of funding for years. In actual fact, this was part of the strategy to undermine us — to try to starve us of funding, when we should have been getting it in bucket loads for the fabulous positive work we were doing.

We decided to focus our resources and co-ordinate a few, high-profile events, including concerts (see Teapot's piece), debates and exhibitions. The Opening Day Carnival Parade and Fun Day were two that involved all ages and areas. We were energized and keen to engage with anyone and everyone. We were proud of who we were, confident and not afraid to engage. We weren't arrogant — we were who we were and we were sick and tired of the way in which we were portrayed by the media as responsible for everything that was wrong. We wanted people who didn't know us to have an opportunity to find out about us. More than that, the festival became our opportunity to show the world who we were and what we could do together. We wanted to counter the negative image, and again, Brit propaganda strategy, which was out to undermine us across the globe. We did this from the ground up. We embraced community and culture. We put it out there. The message was, 'if you live here, enjoy the festival. If you don't live here, come and enjoy the festival and meet us: fáilte – you're welcome.' Many hundreds of people took us at our word and came along for the fun, dance, craic and the talking. We were opening doors and minds, strengthening old relationships and creating new ones.

Alongside the debate and song was the theatre/drama group. Plays were put to paper. Actors were found — they had been there all along! The drama group was formed. Stories were told and then told again on stage. Real life drama walked the floorboards and it was truly brilliant. (Hopefully someone from this group will pen this, as this was their thing, and unfortunately some of the key people involved in this have since died.) People laughed and cried. Venues were packed to the gills. Standing room only. This was another way of opening doors, breaking down artistic/cultural barriers within our own community and beyond. Drama didn't have to be considered 'high art'. The people who do it, define it. If you can't connect with it, what good is it? It had to mean something to you. If it didn't, what was the point? If we had tried to bring in something that was considered 'high art' and it didn't hold meaning in our lives, it wouldn't have worked. Everything was about who we were, what we'd been through and where we were at. Of course, we could invite big names to concerts (if we were lucky) but other forms of culture had, first and foremost, to come from and be rooted inside our community.

We invited local artists to exhibit their work and we supported local mural artists to showcase their work on the walls of the Falls and elsewhere. Poets and writers were asked to come in and do readings and workshops. Food artists were drawn in to an International Food Fair, which went along with the International Day. We had visitors from the Basque Country, England, America, Corsica and elsewhere.

Laurence McKeown and Brian Campbell organized a film festival, which has since become The Belfast Film Festival. Féile was the birth of many babies — literally! Éigse an Phobail, our winter school, was another development. We had the Prisoners' Day too. This was vitally important in West Belfast: many, many families were affected by the conflict, with family members in jail over long periods of time. The Prisoners' Day was as much a part of the festival as the Opening Day. POWs and ex-POWs had a lot to offer in terms of comradeship, endurance, resistance, wisdom, wit and reflection. They were another source of sincere community pride and inspiration.

As we took care of meeting deadlines and pulling our collective hair out at the same time, pressure was always intense. We developed a funding strategy, which amounted, more or less, to knocking on every door to see what we could get: money, support, resources. If it helped, it was counted. We shared information with groups, be it about funding from Belfast City Council or potential trust funds. We secured sponsors for some of the big-name events. We coordinated press releases and did our bloody best to get the message out there: West Belfast Community Festival is alive and kicking.

We carried out — or rather, got Geraldine McAteer, Ruth Taillon and Niamh Flanagan to work on — an economic appraisal. What's that? I soon learned it was an exercise aimed at identifying what the economic benefit of the festival was: what was its potential to make money and create jobs for our community and for Belfast, and could it be calculated? They soon told us all about it. Everyone had an angle and everyone had work to do. While some of us set about organising and planning and making the festival happen, others could see the bigger picture and were helping us to see it too.

We pulled in anyone and everyone we could think of who had a talent, especially those that thought they had none! The door was open to anyone who wanted to be involved. We answered the phone, followed up calls, stayed in touch, and when we weren't fighting … we were laughing. It was high pressure, but certainly worth it at the time and, in retrospect, worth much more than we imagined possible.

The festival reflected the broad politics of the area. Gerry Adams, one of the founders, pushed boundaries and buttons, took chances, stuck his neck out, and made things happen for Féile. Whatever contacts he had, he used. This was all happening in the early days of the peace process, when Sinn Féin and their supporters and voters were regarded as people who could be denied their rights and dignity. They could be disregarded and excluded. Gerry used whatever credit he had for the benefit of the festival. Don't forget that the British broadcasting ban was imposed on the party until 1994. So, fair play to those people who supported us and really did stand by the vision we had. They broke down barriers and helped to break the deadlock. Adams had conviction, vision and confidence. It became infectious. As the working group coordinating the festival, we could put anything on the table, and did; we were free to explore without feeling inhibited or feeling that you were breaking rank. Instead, we were breaking new ground, pushing out boundaries, making and creating space for exchanges that no-one could have imagined possible back then.

I am from Ballymurphy and so extremely proud of that. I must honestly admit that the best of Féile was all of it! I loved what I was doing. It was pressure and stress, but it was also comradeship and a privilege. It was doing something exciting with other enthusiastic and committed people — making things happen. We laughed, cried, fought, drank, hugged and then some. I am so very thankful, really, for this experience. Go raibh maith agat Siobhán, Angela, Tony, Gerry, Danny, Aidan, Geraldine, Laurence and Brian.

Féile: where humanity can flourish

MÍCHEAL MAC GIOLLA GHUNNA

Sometime in late spring, 1988, I was invited to a meeting in the Falls Community Council (FCC) offices in the strange little bungalow on Kennedy Way roundabout. Gerry Adams wanted to discuss organising a community festival for West Belfast.

At that time we were still emerging from one of those dark and intense periods of the conflict, beginning with the killing of three IRA volunteers in Gibraltar and ending with the deaths of two British soldiers in Andersonstown — and with the days marked by funeral after funeral. People were tired and emotionally bruised, even those of us too young to know any other life. In addition, the British establishment had launched a vicious propaganda attack on the community in West Belfast, aided and abetted by the political opportunism of anti-republican elements in Ireland, including the Dublin government, the SDLP and the Catholic Church. The community of West Belfast, which had lost so many in those short weeks, was labelled a 'terrorist community', thereby preparing the ground for further repression.

The community response? Let's have a festival! And so, to the FCC offices and around a dozen activists packed into a small room. The energy, ambition and imagination were incredible. We had visions of rivalling the Notting Hill Carnival or the Freedom Festival in Jamaica. Instead of Bob Marley, however, we ended up with Mickey Marley and his horse-drawn roundabout (and he didn't let anyone on for free). We wanted to showcase West Belfast as a talented, radical and compassionate community struggling for freedom, justice and peace — 'twenty years on, unbowed, unbroken, undefeated', as the wall mural on the lower Falls proclaimed. For me it was also part of the Broad Front initiative — to maximise the progressive forces against injustice and repression and to broaden support for a republican, rights-based Ireland.

The activists at the meeting were practical, let's-just-do-it people and quickly turned the grand vision into actions and responsibilities. Deirdre McManus would coordinate the festival and contact community groups and local district festivals. Teapot, Hector, Tony Carlisle, Jim Moody were to organise some head-liners. Danny from Belfast Exposed would organise an exhibition. Someone would contact Robert Ballagh to judge a mural competition, and someone else would tie in with Ulick O'Connor and Tomás Mac Anna, who together had a new play, *Executions*, in the pipeline. I was assigned to assist Deirdre (I may have even been given a title of Assistant Coordinator).

Deirdre and I spent days going around community groups, local activists and street-festival organisers trying to get them involved. Many people were very positive and understood the logic of the West Belfast Festival immediately. Others took some persuading — concerned about the work commitment or loyal to their local street events. Some groups wanted to know what they would get out of it — did we have money, people to help them? A stalwart of the Irish language community wanted to know what we would be organising in Irish, whereas I was asking him what role the Irish language community could play in the festival initiative. Apart from a few big events, we were not organising a festival for the people; *they* were organising their own festival. (A few years later, the great and the good organised a 'community' festival for the people of the Shankill, which seemed to me to miss the point.) Our idea was to put all the various activities that occurred in the August week into one programme to celebrate the talents and spirit of the West Belfast community.

Beyond our own community, it was difficult to get much support. The prop-aganda campaign against 'republican' West Belfast had frightened people from linking their names with us. It is to the eternal credit of those who did come — Robert Ballagh, Brush Shiels, Ulick O'Connor, Tomás Mac Anna and others — that they were prepared to break the political and ideological siege. However, we took advantage of every opportunity to contact any and everyone. For instance, we heard that the singer Billy Bragg would be appearing at a lunchtime talk in the Belfast Centre for the Unemployed in Donegall St. It was decided that I should go down and speak to him about taking part in the festival. I wasn't sure what kind of reception I would get. 'Just brass-neck it,' advised Teapot. That was the approach to most things. On this occasion it wasn't very successful — I approached Billy uninvited, explained who I was, handed him a letter I'd prepared, then beat a hasty retreat under the watchful (baleful?) stare of minders and trade union officials. We never heard back from him.

We tried to get some media traction, with mixed results. I did an interview with Martin O'Hagan of the *Sunday World* in a bedroom of the Europa Hotel, which they were using as an office. 'Any Workers' Party involvement?' he asked. I told him that I wasn't sure — there were a lot of people involved. The jazz musician and radio presenter Jackie Flavelle asked, 'Any jazz involvement?'

In my naivety I replied that that jazz bands were too dear — which was true (over £500). I did an interview standing outside the FCC offices, for the local BBC TV teatime news, in which the questioning, if I remember correctly, was about the political context of having a festival in West Belfast. UTV, on the other hand, interviewed me on their summer festival round-up slot.

We also had a meeting with the *Irish News* about sponsoring the festival. They offered what we believed was a paltry £200, and we rejected it. However, they made sure to mention the festival on their signs outside newsagents on the Falls Road — the *Irish News 'for all your festival coverage'*. The *Andersonstown News* was more positive however.

All these efforts gradually came together in an impressive programme of events, from big concerts to street parties, from sports' competitions to political debates and exhibitions. We had a launch in Conway Mill, with Irish coffees all round — except that there was no whiskey left when it came to my turn (I'm still annoyed!). It was a hectic week for us all. There were red heart stickers with 'I love West Belfast' everywhere. One of my highlights was accompanying Robert Ballagh around all the murals, my favourite being the one of Nelson Mandela ('Happy Birthday, Comrade') painted by Sinn Féin Youth across from Sevastopol St. In the end, at a lecture in the Roddy's, Ballagh gave top prize to Gerry 'Mo Chara' Kelly's depiction, in Springhill Avenue, of the Celtic god Nuada. Later we ended up in the marquee, on waste ground outside the PD club in Andersonstown. A storm raged around us, furiously shaking the 'tent', flickering the lights and eventually snapping one of the struts holding the tent up. Welcome to the West Belfast Festival!

The play *Executions* by Ulick O'Connor and directed by Tomás Mac Anna was both poignant and thought-provoking — a real coup for the festival. I'd never seen a photographic exhibition before and I appreciated the efforts of Belfast Exposed and others in bringing this experience to West Belfast. The political debate was organised by the '68 Committees who were examining how far we'd come since 1968 and how we could take the demands of the Civil Rights movement forward.

The saddest event was the annual vigil for the victims of plastic bullets. John Downes had been shot dead only four years earlier and the families of all the victims, especially of the children killed, continued to struggle for justice. The festival in 1988 was a big party to raise community morale. It was a showcase for talent and imagination, a platform for ideas and debate. But it was also a reminder that this was a community placed at the heart of a conflict that they had not chosen but which they responded to with courage and resilience, hope, humour and positivity. The festival became another of those small but significant steps towards framing our own future in our own way.

Féile: where humanity can flourish: *Mícheal Mac Giolla Ghunna*

In 1989 I worked on publicity for the festival. In 1990 I was imprisoned but continued to receive the Féile an Phobail programme and the posters (works of art in themselves, one of which adorned the wall of my cell). The H-Blocks were a hive of cultural activity — education, literature, drama, music — because the republican struggle is ultimately about creating the political circumstances in which human society can flourish. In 1995 I was in H4, where a group of us were attempting to adapt Bobby Sands's poetry — 'The Crime of Castlereagh', 'Diplock Court' and 'H-Block Torture Mill' — for the stage, using the approach of Augusto Boal, the 'Theatre of the Oppressed'. With the invaluable guidance and support of Tom Magill from the Community Arts Forum, we eventually completed what we believed was a credible production. We took it 'on tour' around the other blocks, performing to a very appreciative albeit captive audience. We then received an invitation from Féile to perform it in August 1996, as part of the festival. The other members of the group were in a position to apply for a few days' parole, as they were nearing the end of their sentences. I had more time to go and could not get parole. We tried a couple of other POWs in my role, but it was not working. The Camp OC (Officer Commanding) and myself spoke to prison governors without success. Finally, Féile came up with an imaginative and generous solution — the festival was not about a week in August, it was about a celebration of talents, ideas and artistic expression, which could happen at any time. So the festival was extended until I could get parole.

One morning, in September 1996, I was released on parole from the H-Blocks and was driven straight to St Agnes's Hall in Andersonstown to rehearse for that night's performance. It was a bizarre and bewildering experience to be, after breakfast in the Blocks, suddenly back in the outside world and for such an occasion. Introduced by Gerry Adams, we performed our work that night to over 500 people and to a rapturous reception (as might be expected). For me, I was back at the festival.

Féile an Phobail – 30 years a-growing

GERRY ADAMS

I didn't get to any Féile events in 2017. That's a first. Truth is, I was too tired. Martin's death. Two elections. Two USA trips in July. Constituency duties in the Dáil and in Louth. Talks or what passed for talks at Stormont. It all takes time and effort.

So I decided to forgo Féile this year. I missed a very wonderful series of events. I was particularly sore not to get to the RFJ's Plastic Bullet picket. Another first. But I followed it all on Twitter. Especially Clara Reilly. A mighty woman. Battling on. Never giving up. Emma Groves and Clara were never beaten. Never will be.

Féile is great. Taking a step back from it all is a very good way to appreciate how great it really is. So once again well done and thanks to Sam and Kevin and Angela and Harry Beag and all the women and men of the current brilliant, energetic and ever-resourceful Féile team. That includes Ciarán Morrison, who is leaving after 17 years of Féile adventures. And Ciarán eile, who keeps us honest.

Back in the days before Féile an Phobail, West Belfast was a different country. Under military occupation. Censored. Community structures subjected to political vetting. Discrimination rampant. Everyone was related to or knew someone who was a political prisoner. Neighbours' sons and daughters. No state funding whatsoever for Irish language education. Little for Gaelic games. Neighbourhoods subjected to counter-insurgency measures. Betrayed by church hierarchies and by the great and the good. Including Dublin. Especially Dublin. Community leaders and political representatives targeted by British state-sponsored death squads.

Republican West Belfast was a community in rebellion. We still are. Back then, we were deeply invested in a culture of resistance against occupation and oppression. Many of our battles were defensive. Underground. But we were in transition. Our culture of resistance was becoming a culture of change.

Of reconquest. But there were too few platforms for this. The republican community of West Belfast was hemmed in. Under the cosh. Unbowed and unbroken. But needing an outlet for our positive energy and imagination. And vision.

The killings at Gibraltar of three outstanding West Belfast citizens, Volunteers Mairead Farrell, Seán Savage and Dan McCann, and especially the establishment's vile demonisation of their community — our community — was a tipping point. A lesser people could not have survived the decades of vicious insults, lies and invective. But this onslaught and the attacks on their funerals and the other funerals and deaths of Caoimhín Mac Brádaigh, Thomas McErlean and John Murray which followed, including the two British soldiers, became a catalyst for that culture of change to find a platform. Féile an Phobail was a result of that. We were telling our detractors to f... off. We knew who we were. We were no better than anyone else. But we were no worse.

So Féile was our answer. Our alternative. It became the forum or forums for local artists, poets, photographers, singers, dramatists, dancers, painters, chancers, writers, talkers, sports people and spoofers to strut their stuff. To yell yahoo! In harmony. To give licence for hope and creativity and cheerfulness and positivity. To reclaim our space. To create space for others. To enjoy ourselves. To say this is who we are. Not a terrorist community. But a patriotic, resourceful, intelligent, cheerful, confident, caring and hopeful gathering of men and women looking to the future and prepared to imagine that that future could be fair and inclusive. And happy. Capable of making our own music. Of shaping and creating our own vision.

Féile was also an invite for other progressives to join us. And they did. Playwrights. Painters. Singers. Musicians. Actors. Actresses. Activists from other struggles. Other political views. Other traditions. Boy bands and girl bands. Writers. Orchestras. Rap artists. Sean-nós singers. Hip-hoppers. Rappers. Céilí dancers. Movers and shakers. Stilt walkers. Discreet walzers. Tango dancers. Talkers. Walkers. Citizens with disabilities. Old people. Children. Youth. Wannabe youths. Cooks. Cranks. Fly boys from the love comics. Loose men. Delinquent pensioners. Dog lovers. Dogs. Glamorous grannies.

Some are coming to Féile still. Now part of the Féile family. Marie Jones brought her plays. She nurtured a theatrical undercurrent which took its own communal stories and experiences and gave them dramatic form. Pam Brighton mentored local writers and stage designers and sound engineers. Citizens who were never in a theatre flocked to parish halls, local schools, community centres and GAA clubs to be uplifted and moved to tears or cheers. Field Day included the Féile in its tours. Stephen Rea brought Oscar to life. Ulick O'Connor and the late Tomás MacAnna gave us *Executions*. Dan Gordon gave us *A Night in November*. The list is endless. A new generation of young artistes blossomed. They are still captivating us with their art. Local performers, writers. Bi-lingual drama at its best. Communal tales with universal themes.

Robert Ballagh arrived to acknowledge the artistic beauty and integrity of our fledgling mural painters. Where previously the painting of political graffiti was liable to incur RUC harassment or worse, no one could stop you painting a gable wall if the householder was content to have their gable transformed by Mo Chara or Danny D, Martie or their legions of fledgling Jim Fitzpatricks. And Jim came as well to praise their masterpieces.

So did Gerry Keenan, with orchestras to beat the band. *The Sky's The Limit* opened for The Ulster Orchestra. Peadar Ó Riada brought *An Cor Cullaigh*. Eddie Keenan sang 'I Was There'. Seán Maguire enthralled us with his fiddle magic. Mícheál Ó Súilleabháin with his piano. Terry Enright brought us up the Black Mountain. The Falls Park hosted An Poc Fada. The Bobby Sands Cup challenged soccer teams. The Mairead Farrell Tournament did the same for camógs. Aidan Creen and Terry Goldsmith opened up The Bog Meadows. Tom Hartley started his graveyard tours. Féile opened our own radio station. If we were blocked from other media, why not start our own? Hector McNeill and Tea Pot footered at that for a while. Donnacha Rynne made his debut there. Fergus Ó hÍr dabbled in Irish-language radio broadcasting. Raidió Fáilte was born. Ag fás fós.

Martin Sheen came to visit. And later Michael Moore. And many, many more. President Mary Robinson defied both the British and Irish governments and visited us with the active encouragement of Inez McCormack, Eileen Howell and other sisters. Mary McAleese, no stranger, was later to make the same journey also as President.

And those who censored us? We reached out to them and invited them to talk and to listen to us. We welcomed detractors and other naysayers along with ordinary decent citizens to West Belfast Talks Back. Discussion groups, debates and lectures flourished under the leaderships of Jake Jackson, Paddy Kelly, Majella McCloskey, Siobhán O'Hanlon, Carol Jackson, Bill Rolston, Danny Morrison and Jim Gibney. Danny also pioneered Scribes at The Rock and the odd time in The West Club, and brought authors from far and near.

Exhibitions blossomed everywhere. Quilts. Photos. Posters. Drawings. Paintings. Sculptures. H-Block comms. The West Belfast Film Festival brought Stephen Fry to visit. He was amazed at the grey threatening awfulness of the Barracks opposite Milltown Cemetery and delighted by the welcome he got in McEnaney's. Seamus Heaney came as well. His first time back in St Thomas's since he taught there. A memorable day with Jimmy Ellis at Sam Thompson's graveside in the City Cemetery and later in St Mary's.

And singing? We sang like angels. With Planxty. Anúna. Frances Black. Mary Black. The Buena Vista Social Club. The Wolfe Tones. Bríd Keenan. Altan. Brian Kennedy. Shane MacGowan. Davy Spillane. Dolores Keane. Mick Hanley. Jimmy Yamaha. A Welsh miners' choir. Brush Shiels. Jimmy McCarthy. Fra McCann. Floyd Westerman. St Agnes's Choral Society. Tony McMahon and Noel Hill. Christy. UB40. Brian Moore. Noírín Ní Riain. Tony Carlisle, Flair, Jim Moody became friends of the stars. High flyers.

For years we survived without funding. Our leaders included Deirdre McManus, Siobhán, Danny Power, Seán Paul O'Hare, Geordie Murdoch, Caitríona Ruane, Niamh Flanagan, Geraldine McAteer, Ciaran Quinn, Aidan McAteer, Ciaran Kearney, Deirdre Mackle, Margaret McKernan, Deirdre Walsh, Maura Brown, Chrissie Keenan and Bridie. And countless others. Many worked in a voluntary capacity. The *Andersonstown News* was always an ally. And the local Irish-language community. And Springhill, the main concert venue for years. Right in the centre of the war zone. No one else would have done it with such panache.

Now the Féile is Ireland's foremost community festival. Despite the best efforts of those who lorded it over us thirty years ago. I am sure the history of this will all be chronicled. It needs to be. Memory is important. So too is the telling of our own stories. That's what Féile is about. Writing the future while righting the past.

But the arts needs proper, dedicated core funding. Local sponsors have kept faith. We are grateful to them, but the Féile team survives on a shoe string. Could it be better? Of course. But almost 30 years later, Féile is still one of the best things I was ever involved with. Its success is a great credit to everyone who was or is associated in any way with this outstanding communal celebration. Not all the names are included here. That is not intentional. So if you're left out or if you know somebody who is left out, shout! This is only my flawed, hurried little recollection. Write your own. Send it to *Andytown News*. Or the Féile office. With photos if you have them. Maybe, as we celebrate thirty years a-growing, some of us will find the time to write a list of all the Féile leaders and champions and do a Féile Thirty Years On Birthday ReUnion. Just to remember and say go raibh míle maith agaibh go léir.

An Féile abú!

By hook or by crook

Fachtna Ó Ceallaigh

My mother always said that good things come in small packages, but that thought was very far from my mind as I stepped out of the lift in Jurys Hotel, Ballsbridge, Dublin, on what was for me a fateful day in 1988, and saw in front of me a couple of what can only be described as very short men accompanied by one or two others of much greater stature.

The mostly denim-clad motley crew turned out to be Jimmy Teapot McMullan, Hector McNeill, Tony Carlisle and Jim Moody. They were actually looking for Sinéad O'Connor, whom I managed at the time, but they, being poor unfortunates, ended up with me.

30 years later I can hand-on-heart safely say that I got the better part of the deal. Led by Jimmy, I got an explanation on that day of the purposes behind the newly formed Féile an Phobail/West Belfast Community Festival. Thanks to their articulacy and passion, I immediately completely understood the reasoning behind the festival, the need to channel the energies of the collective communities into a positive message of self-sufficiency, joy and laughter amidst the day-to-day realities of the war, the desire to replace the endless images of barricades, burning buses and rioting youths that, year-on-year during the august anniversaries, served only the oppressors' purposes.

Given that Ms O'Connor was not of a mind to commit herself to performing at the festival, I offered myself and whatever I could do. I ended up making numerous visits to West Belfast, learning something new every time and meeting absolutely incredible people such as the Keenan family, Brendan Hughes and many others. I laughed my way around the streets of Iarthar Bhéal Feirste with Jimmy and his pals, watched pints pile up in front of me — a non-drinker — in all sorts of bars and pubs, and ended up listening to often but not always drunken ramblings about anything and everything at four o'clock in the morning. And I loved every minute of it.

And somehow a festival formed. The likes of Mo Chara borrowed 40-foot trailers that became a stage in Springhill. Andytown Leisure Centre was a slightly more 'normal' venue, although I did observe the odd bout of fisticuffs on the door when somebody would feel entitled enough to force their way in to whatever gig was on without paying. The combined forces of Teapot and others always successfully repelled the invaders. And then there was the fancy-dress dog competition/parade one year, when teapot and Annemarie's dog merrily trotted down to Ballymurphy resplendent in a tutu, fearlessly passing a joint Brit/RUC patrol while on the run having bitten a peeler a couple of days previously.

A year or two later, I got the chance to spend a bit of time in Los Angeles with Everlast, the main rapper in the group House of Pain who were at that stage hugely popular with their anthem 'Jump Around'. He was and is a good man with Irish heritage and I floated the idea of the band performing at the Féile, having given him some kind of feel for the reasoning behind the festival. He made the commitment that they would play and with great excitement I duly reported the news to Jimmy Teapot. I arranged to see Everlast and his two hip-hop compadres, Danny Boy and DJ Lethal, at the Trip to Tipp in Thurles during that summer.

A large delegation arrived in Thurles from West Belfast and by hook or by crook and with a few guest passes being thrown over fencing to those still outside, we managed to get everybody in backstage with the lads, including Tony, Flair and others. We sat with Danny Boy, enjoying the hospitality of the free drinks and grub and nodded our heads agreeably when he announced that he was going to get the Amsterdam chapter of the Hells Angels to escort him, and presumably his bandmates, on their Harleys into the welcoming arms of muintir Bhéal Feirste. 'We're gonna tear shit up', he promised. The rumble in the jungle would have nothing on this for sure. Sadly, as it turned out Everlast's father became very ill, he had to fly back to LA, and the thrilling, hilarious prospect of a House of Pain mega-jump up in Springhill became a thing of fantasy.

The broadcasting ban on Sinn Féin and republican voices was in full effect in those days. Fortunately, while living in London, I got to know the people who set up the first black-owned pirate radio station, called DBC or Dread Broadcasting Corporation. The main man, Daddy Lepke, agreed to introduce me to people who made transmitters, which were the essential ingredient, and so, at a reasonable cost, I acquired three of them with the idea of enabling pirate stations to be set up in Belfast, Derry and somewhere along the border, thus bypassing the ban. Through fair means — I think — and not foul, the goods were transported to the occupied territories and a while later I found myself on a rooftop with Lepke, at the top of the Whiterock Road, positioning an aerial to facilitate the future transmission of whatever the local community wanted to say over the airwaves during Féile an Phobail. I recall Lepke was worried about fingerprints and the like but we got him in and out of there without any bother.

There are plenty of other stories, but actually they are mere anecdotes. What is striking is that the creative genius of Jimmy, Hector, Brendan, Mo Chara, Tony and others spawned an idea and then hustled and harried and gambled to turn it into a living, breathing thing involving thousands of people, all of them uplifted by their contributions and participation. It was, at that time, truly a people's event and whatever it is now, thirty years later, it must always strive to remember the true meaning of its name — Féile an Phobail/the West Belfast Community Festival.

And please, one more thing; promise never, ever again to spend eighty grand booking T'pau.

Pictures of the Upper Springfield Community Festival, August 1973, *courtesy of Ciarán De Baróid and Springhill Community House.*

Loyalist gunman, Michael Stone, firing at the mourners as they give chase. *Picture courtesy of Pacemaker Press.*

The coffins of IRA members Dan McCann, Mairead Farrell and Seán Savage being carried on the Andersonstown Road, Belfast. *Picture courtesy of Pacemaker Press.*

Graveside cortege as loyalist Michael Stone's first hand grenade lands beside mourners. *Picture courtesy of Seán Murray.*

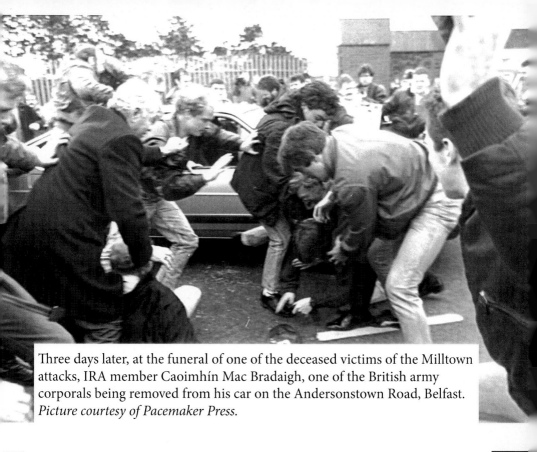

Three days later, at the funeral of one of the deceased victims of the Milltown attacks, IRA member Caoimhín Mac Bradaigh, one of the British army corporals being removed from his car on the Andersonstown Road, Belfast. *Picture courtesy of Pacemaker Press.*

Renowned artist Robert Ballagh judging the mural competition for the first Féile in August 1988. With him are Seamus Downey (14) and Elizabeth Connelly (15) from the Lower Falls. This solidarity mural of South African leader Nelson Mandela, who was still incarcerated at the time, came in second place. *Picture courtesy of Bill Rolston.*

Jimmy McMullan and Hector McNeill at the first Féile parade in Dunville Park, August 1988. *Picture courtesy of Jimmy McMullan.*

Concert in full flow in Andersonstown Marquee, which Jimmy McMullan refers to in his piece. *Picture Courtesy of Seán McKiernan.*

A street party in Unity Flats, August 1988. *Picture courtesy of Seán McKiernan.*

A famous Springhill guider race with associated water fight.
Picture courtesy of Gerard 'Mo Chara' Kelly.

Springhill residents dressed in Braveheart attire at the Féile 'Party in the Park' after marching on the Henry Taggart RUC Barracks, 1995.
Picture courtesy of Gerard 'Mo Chara' Kelly.

Concert venue at Springhill – art covered makeshift lorry as concert stage. *Picture courtesy of Gerard 'Mo Chara' Kelly.*

Packed concert at Springhill venue. *Picture courtesy of Seán McKiernan.*

The JustUs women's theatre group, together with republican prisoners in Portlaoise Prison, having performed their 1996 play *Just a Prisoners Wife*. *Picture courtesy of Chrissie Mhic Siacais.*

Gerry Adams and then Taoiseach Albert Reynolds meet to officially open Teach na Féile, in March 1997, during a crucial period in the Irish peace process. They are pictured here along with Féile Director Caitríona Ruane. *Picture courtesy of Féile an Phobail.*

The St Patrick's Day parade to proceed to Belfast City Hall, March 1998. The parade was spearheaded by Féile, *Picture courtesy of Mal McCann.*

Hollywood actor Martin Sheen with Féile activists having come over to attend the West Belfast Film Festival, 1998. *Picture courtesy of Seán McKernan.*

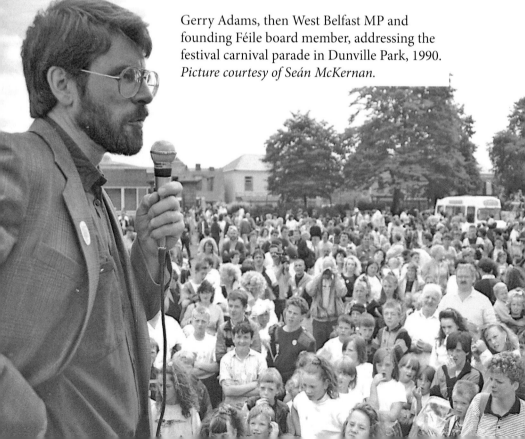

Gerry Adams, then West Belfast MP and founding Féile board member, addressing the festival carnival parade in Dunville Park, 1990. *Picture courtesy of Seán McKernan.*

Féile carnival parade coming up the Falls Road, August 1995. *Picture courtesy of The Irish News.*

alachy McCambridge, Brendan McMahon, erry Adams and Veronica Brown, outside e Triple/Féile FM radio station, August 98. *Picture courtesy of Veronica Brown.*

Mural artist Michael Doherty working on a Guernica bombing commemorative mural, on the International Wall, for Féile 2009. *Picture courtesy of Bill Rolston.*

The late environmental campaigner, Terry Enright, takes his annual Black Mountain Féile walk, August 1998. *Picture courtesy of Féile an Phobail.*

Danny Morrison interviewing the writer Paul Laverty at the annual Féile literary event, Scribes at the Rock, August 2016. *Picture courtesy of Belfast Media group.*

Tom Hartley takes his Belfast City Cemetery tour, August 2009. *Picture courtesy of Féile an Phobail.*

LGBTQ campaigners with their banner at the Féile parade, August 2002. *Picture courtesy of Bill Rolston.*

Members (four of them contributors to this memoir collection) of the Féile Debates and Discussions group, with Nobel Prize-winning Irish poet Seamus Heaney at the 2010 Féile. From left: Paddy Kelly, Danny Morrison, Seamus Heaney, Carol Moore, Jim Gibney and Bill Rolston. *Picture courtesy of Bill Rolston.*

Ballymurphy massacre campaigners during the 2012 August Féile on their annual march. *Picture courtesy of Féile an Phobail.*

The crowd at the August 2015 UB40 concert in the Féile marquee. *Picture courtesy of Féile an Phobail.*

An aerial shot of the 2017 Féile marquee. *Picture courtesy of Bayview Media.*

From political activist to tour guide and author

Tom Hartley

It was my role in the Belfast Republican Press Centre at 170a Falls Road, where I worked in the early 1970s, that indirectly laid the foundations for my role in the West Belfast Festival. In those early years, journalists visiting Belfast would often ask for a tour of some of the British Army bases scattered throughout the Falls. What began as a visit to a small number of British Army installations slowly grew as I began to include the history of the local area. In between barracks, I added the events of the 1920s, an analysis of the Northern State and the lives of historical figures who were born and lived in the Falls. All of this inside a running commentary on the causes and impact of the conflict, unfolding at that time in the streets around us. So, by 1988 and the emergence of the festival, I had the structure of a ready-made tour, which had evolved in the previous 15 years.

The first tours were in buses, borrowed from the Irish Republican Prisoners' Welfare group, who organised the transport to the various prisons. During the early festivals, the tours ran on a Monday, Wednesday and Friday. As the festival developed, the demand for the tours increased, and eventually they were running from Monday through to Friday.

These bus tours later developed into a walking tour of the City and Milltown cemeteries. A combined tour of both cemeteries was my way of tapping into the complexity of our Belfast history. In the City Cemetery, the history of Belfast as an industrial centre of Empire can be found on the headstones of the leading industrialists, who made the city the Silicon Valley of its day. These headstones also remind us of the cultural complexity of the Belfast Protestant community. One example of this is the Reverend Richard Rutledge Kane, a Church of Ireland Rector and a leading Orangeman in Belfast, who led the opposition to Gladstone's first Home Rule Bill. On his headstone he is described as 'A Faithful Pastor, Gifted Orator and Loyal Irish Patriot'. Reputed to be an Irish speaker, he is recorded as being one of the patrons of the Belfast Gaelic League; in the December 1895 issue of the *Gaelic Journal*, he is named as one of its sponsors.

His inscription, which sets his loyalty to the Union inside an Irish patriotic frame, still manages to challenge many visitors to his grave. To the modern political eye, the inscription 'Loyal Irish Patriot' seems to be at odds with our understanding of how the terms 'loyal' and 'Irish' are interpreted in today's political context. The cemetery also contains many family inscriptions of First World War dead, and approximately four hundred graves under the care of the Commonwealth War Grave Commission.

In Milltown Cemetery, the history of the Belfast nationalist community and all of its political manifestations can be found. The inscriptions on headstones tell the story of the republican struggle, and the development of the Catholic community, with its church and educational structure, as it sought to gain a foothold in the predominantly Protestant and unionist city. Conflict-related deaths in this cemetery date from 1886 and the first Home Rule Bill. James McFall, the last harp maker of Belfast, is buried a hundred yards from Cathal O'Byrne, famous for his book *As I Roved Out*. What both cemeteries have in common are thousands of poor, buried in unmarked graves; women hidden from our historical view, soldiers who died for empire, and the complex narrative that tells the story of Belfast.

On reflection, it was inevitable that this interest in history would propel me into committing the historical information, gathered over years of research, into written form. So often, on the walks through the cemeteries, I would be asked 'is there a book on the cemetery'? Eventually, in 2006, *Written in Stone, the History of Belfast City Cemetery* was published, and launched in the Belfast Central Library. It took me another eight years before my second book, *Milltown Cemetery, The History of Belfast, Written in Stone* was launched, as part of Féile an Phobail, in the old assembly hall in St Dominick's school on the Falls Road, on 31 July 2014.

In September 2014, I turned my attention to the history of a small burial ground on Stockman's Lane, which today is known as Balmoral Cemetery. Founded in 1855 by the Rev Henry Cooke and the Rev McKenzie from Malone Presbyterian Church, this small burial ground is packed with the history of Belfast Presbyterianism in the nineteenth century. At the time of writing this article, a manuscript exploring the history of this cemetery is in its first stage of editing, hopefully to be published soon.

How, then, should I interpret the journey from political activist to tour guide and author? The lynchpin that holds this personal narrative together is the founding of the West Belfast Festival in 1988. It was at this juncture of my life that the skills of the political activist were adopted to tell the story of my local community and of the two largest burial grounds in Belfast. This was not such a big gap to cross, going from being an author of political papers to becoming an author of a local history book.

The interpretation of my journey contains another dimension that needs to be recognised: this is the role and creativity of the community I was born into. When I pass a mural on the Falls Road, I am reminded of its hidden meaning to the Falls community. Murals emerged during the hunger strikes of 1980-81, a time of great sadness and darkness in the republican community. In their efforts to capture the events of that period, the young muralists of West Belfast used the gable walls of their streets to convey to the world their inner thoughts on the hunger strikers and to use their creativity against the darkness imposed on them by the political forces that sought to crush the hunger strikers. Likewise with the West Belfast Festival: at a time when the nationalist community of West Belfast was being demonised, the area's political and community activists created the festival as a way of using their creativity against the demonisation imposed upon them. I and the thousands who built the reputation of the festival are the product of that dynamic creativity. We are Féile 30.

From Bramble Folk to Boyzone

Tommy Holland

The first Féile an Phobail in 1988 was an event that would change my life and the lives of many, many others forever, in the best possible way. I can recall us putting together our first float for the parade to Dunville Park. It was called 'Cinderella'. Then we started clearing a derelict site in Springhill for the concerts and the children's fun days. We had the band Bramble Folk on the back of a coal lorry and discos mixed with fun events, from children's fancy dress to pets' fancy dress to fancy-dress football matches.

During one of these days, a large British Army foot patrol entered Springhill and I remember the look of bewilderment on their faces and the utter panic as they were confronted with pet dogs dressed in baby grows barking at them, with one Alsatian dog wearing boxing shorts and boxing gloves tied around its neck. They would then turn the corner and walk straight into us 22 Springhill footballers dressed as Batman, Robin, and the Hulk, with some of the lads wearing suspenders and wigs. Dressed as a Viking, I was the goalkeeper, and some of the lads had wigs on and horrible make up as they mockingly blew kisses at the new young squaddies, who probably thought they just walked into the Twilight Zone instead of a militarised zone!

So, amidst hardship and heartbreak during the conflict, we found a way to lift our spirits and our people's spirits with the Féile. In the following years, Springhill entered loads of floats and won loads of Féile parade float trophies, providing a good-humoured challenge and competition between areas and groups each year in West Belfast, from Falls, Andersonstown, Lenadoon etc.

Over the years the Springhill Féile group consisted of Hector Heath's team, made up of local people, and our artist-in-residence, Gerard 'Mo Chara' Kelly, who all built the site and staging, and painted magnificent murals on them that would be just as good as any staging you would see at any major concert site.

The Springhill Youth Action Group was set up to ensure our children and families were provided with daily events. The best thing that happened, however, was that the whole estate got involved in the Féile events, welcoming thousands of people into the Springhill estate. Friends and the best of neighbours worked tirelessly to provide this escape from the troubles that were ongoing on a weekly and sometimes a daily basis.

So we built it in our wee estate and they did come in their thousands and enjoyed much more than Bramble Folk, playing in Springhill Avenue. We had Shane MacGowan, Brush Sheils, the Century Steel Band, Black 47 — who sang a song called Fuck Columbus at 3.00am in the morning — which was class. We had the Love Dogs and a fantastic local band with Cubb McCullough, The Imposters, who always brought the roof down (even though we didn't have a roof).

We held our community karaoke nights in the back of Corpus Christi Chapel and Paddy Dillon and Crooksy, who were the DJs at night, did sets at our children's discos during the day. We held fun tug-of-war against Ballymurphy Ex-POWs and had some of the biggest water-balloon fights ever, against West Belfast.

We built our floats that will live long in the memory: Alien Space Ships, Sister Act, Darby O'Gill, Native Americans, Aladdin, Save The Black Mountain Campaign with Terry Enright, and Braveheart — dressed in our kilts and blue face paint carrying 18ft bamboos with the Scottish flag on them and armed with large wooden hammers and swords. On that occasion, we went to the Henry Taggert British Army Barracks at the top of our street and, of course, lifted our kilts and mooned at those invaders manning the sentry boxes. The expressions on their faces were a scream.

Then we went and joined the Éire Nua Flute band and invaded the Falls Park at the opening of the Féile, stealing Gerry Adams of the stage half way through his speech, as you do. It's no wonder Springhill declared itself Ireland's 33rd county on Féile FM Radio during one of the August Féiltí.

For a few years, I then got voluntarily involved in the management committee of Féile an Phobail. Working with the great staff and committee was fantastic. I worked along with Chrissie Mhic Siacais, helping local groups provide street parties and fun activities in their areas, building the first-day parade, promoting and highlighting the Féile. I then got asked by Mart Holland and Gerard 'Hodgies' to get involved in the Triple FM radio, which later became Féile FM. This I absolutely loved. I walked into the station and we were to go on after Fra Coogan. Fra was finishing up and asked us live on air who we were before we went on. We hadn't thought of any name, so Cubb Mc Cullough just said 'The Village Eejits', and the craic was mighty every time we went on. A good friend of mine, Tambo McNeil, who worked with me in Springhill Youth Group and at the Festival, was a great impersonator and as a Village Eejit on the radio was hilariously funny. People would set their friends and neighbours up, giving us their phone numbers, and we phoned them live on air pretending to be the school board or a politician.

We developed a show called Superstar on Féile FM, which was a bit like X Factor on the radio, and this attracted thousands of listeners to vote for their favourite singer who would win the chance to sing on stage before one of the main Féile acts at the afternoon young-people's concerts. I remember Girls Aloud were about to go on and our wee singer was on first and they were gobsmacked, not just by the loud reaction of the crowd, but by our superstar winner's singing talent. But one of the most hairs-on-the-back-of-your-neck-and-arms-stand-out moments was when Gráinne Mullan won our St Patrick's Day superstar radio competition and sang on stage outside City Hall, at the Féile-organised St Patrick's Day parade. Standing in front of thousands of spectators, her voice carried beautifully down Royal Avenue and around the city centre as she sang 'I will Run Away', by the Corrs, in Irish.

Seriously, I could go on forever about the many happy memories I have of Féile an Phobail, but I will finish where I started, with how the Féile changed my life. In 1988, a person approached us who is now a good friend, mentor and to me a genius and very much a saint. Fr Des Wilson sent for us after the festival was over and said 'right, what are you going to do the rest of the year?' We said, 'work on next year's Féile'. 'What about setting up a Springhill Residents Association?' he replied. 'Look at the state of the houses and there's no play areas for the kids.' So, Fr Des got Joe Reid, who was a teacher and lecturer, to run a committee-management course for us in Springhill Community House. We later became a strong residents' and lobbyist group, and we never looked back. The old Springhill estate was demolished and the houses built to a high standard and a beautiful children's play park is now on the derelict site that the festival was on.

You see, I believe that this was the beauty of those who came up with the idea of the Féile during some heart-breaking and terrible times, when plastic bullets would kill children during August. It was about much more than bringing hordes of people and tourists to the biggest community festival in Europe each August. They gave me and many others the opportunity to shine. Young people I worked with on the Féile and radio are now working in youth and community settings, on radio and television stations, in politics, in the Council, and in Stormont. And I think of wonderful people like Brenda Murphy, who wrote and gave us plays, like the emotional *Ballymurphy Massacre*, the hilariously funny *Night with George* and *Baby it's Cold Outside* — which I have seen four times — and many other great pieces. She is now an internationally acclaimed playwright.

From Bramble Folk to Boyzone: *Tommy Holland*

Féile gave us artists, poets, writers, musicians, singers, community development groups and a thirst for the Irish language, a love of our communities, new friends and great neighbours, Belfast Talks Back, a chance for both our communities and many other communities to talk to each other and get to know each other's perspectives, cultures and beliefs. I put 200 DVDs of a compilation of Springhill Festival events, which Danny Devenny made for me, through the doors of every house in Springhill. I got hugged by some tearful neighbours as their loved ones who had recently passed were on the DVD. I also got shouted at in the street — all in good humour — by current parents and their new families because their kids had great craic seeing their mums and dads as children dancing and singing, in fancy dress, on the floats at the Féile many years ago. This got the community active again about organising a float, fun games and the big wheelie-bin races for their kids.

We still have an Upper Springfield Whiterock Events group and work with and meet regularly with the Féile team — Kevin, Connal, Ciaran and Kevin — providing thousands of families with Halloween, Féile and community events throughout the year, and long may it continue.

So, from Bramble Folk on the back of a coal lorry in Springhill 1988, to Boyzone, Frankie Goes to Hollywood, UB40, the Kaiser Chiefs and other famous acts playing in the Falls Park. The first-day parade, an abundance of various events and a good old water-balloon fight — sure where else would you get it?

Ceiliúradh a dhéanamh don chomóradh

Seán Ó Muireagáin

Tá sé aisteach ag amharc siar anois agus mé ag dul anonn agus an saol athraithe chomh mór sin ó bhí mé óg. Ní raibh mórán le ceiliúradh againn agus mé ag fás aníos — barraíocht le comóradh, ar an drochuair. Ba í Féile an Phobail a chéad thug deis dúinn an t-íochtar a chur ina uachtar agus ceiliúradh a dhéanamh don chomóradh.

Is cuimhin liom nach raibh ann ach cóisir sráide ar an chéad dul síos. Bhailigh muid beagán airgid ó na comharsanaigh agus ceannaíodh milseáin agus sú oráiste agus a leithéid agus thug daoine táblaí amach ar an tsráid. De réir a chéile, cuireadh ceol leis an lá agus d'fhás sin go leoraí mór agus banna ceoil ag seinm ar an chúl.

Chuir sé tús le ré úr, an ceangal a láidriú leis an phobal, go raibh an pobal gníomhach ina bhforbairt féin. Bhí daoine aimsithe ar shráideanna éagsúla agus ghlac siad chucu féin an dualgas sin; rudaí a eagrú don tsráid s'acu féin — agus bhí go leor le déanamh i gcónaí. Creidim féin gur chruthaigh sé daoine áirithe, gur spreagadh iad le hobair phobail a dhéanamh. Tá a fhios agam gur spreag sé mé féin agus, dála an scéil, tá cuid de na daoine go fóill ag tacú le Féile an Phobail go dtí an lá atá inniu ann.

Nuair a tháinig 'Springhill' ar an fhód, d'athraigh sé gach rud. Don chéad uair, bhí an t-aos óg in Iarthar Bhéal Feirste ag dul chuig gigeanna móra oscailte, rud nach ndearna ach fíorbheagán go dtí sin. Ba é seo an rud a thug léargas dúinn go dtiocfadh linne a leithéid a bheith againne fosta, agus tá anois, gan dabht.

Bhí obair le déanamh ar na bóithre chomh maith, ag bailiú airgid gach bliain agus do lámh ag dul isteach i bpócaí an phobail bliain i ndiaidh bliana, ach chothaigh siad muid, níor ligeadh síos muid ariamh, thocail siad go domhain agus thug siad go fial. Daoine deonacha a rinne an obair sin le go léir, cuidithe ó lucht oibre na Féile féin. Níor chuala mé ariamh duine ar bith ag gearán nó ag tabhairt amach fán obair sin — rinneadh í le croí mór maith.

Tá an-mheas agam ar na daoine agus ar an obair a rinne siad na laethanta sin agus tá go fóill bród orm as Féile an Phobail agus iad sin atá go fóill ag soláthar an fhéile is mó pobail san Eoraip. Is moll oibre í féile chomh mór seo a chur i láthair agus imeachtaí de gach cineál a chur ar fáil dúinn mar phobal.

Ní fheictear agus ní aithnítear an obair sin agus í ag tarlú sa chúlra: cruinnithe suaracha leadránacha, a mhairfeadh i bhfad rófhada, agus daoine ag plé gach ábhar na Féile; fochoistí ag plé cúrsaí airgid, cúrsaí ceoil, cúrsaí ealaíon. Rinneadh cuid mhór den obair sin ar bhonn deonach, agus creid uaim é, bhí go leor le déanamh ag na daoine sin taobh amuigh d'obair na Féile. Ach tchítear torthaí na hoibre sin gach bliain san fhómhar agus sa samhradh agus ag amanna eile sa bhliain nach dtugtar faoi deara. Tá rogha ag ár bpobal anois nach raibh againne sna blianta sin fadó, agus is dócha go bhfuil siad millte rud beag anois, ach is ábhar bróid í Féile an Phobail — féile a d'eagraigh ár bpobal féin ar son a bpobail féin.

Ná déanaimis dearmad ar na hoícheanta sin ach an oiread: Brush Shiels, nár thréig sinn ariamh. Shane MacGowan and The Pogues, a d'fhág a lorg orainn go dtí an lá atá inniú ann. The Afro Celts, the Alabama 3. *A Night in November*, an chéad dráma gairmiúil a chonaic mé ariamh, agus a leithéid de dhráma ní dhéanfaidh mé dearmad go deo air sin. Agus go leor leor eile nach iad. Sin iad na cuimhní cinn atá agam anois in áit cuimhní ar an slad agus ar an scrios a rinneadh orainn sna seanlaethanta sin. Tá sé sin i bhfad Éireann níos fearr ná a mhalairt agus na déanaimis dearmad air sin.

Being at Féile: resistance and reconciliation

EILISH ROONEY

What's brilliant about Féile talks is that a burning issue of the day is tackled on the spot by people with strong views backed up by experience and evidence. Have a look online at last year's Debate and Discussion line-up, for example. Where else would you find Amy Goodman telling the story of Democracy Now! and have an opportunity to hear historian Myrtle Hill recount the women's story of the Shankill? You could also have listened to why 'we should understand and not fear Russia' from the former Guardian correspondent, Jonathan Steele. In the same week, people gathered at events where the Ballymurphy families and others considered the question, 'Should British Soldiers be above the Law?' At this event, Louise Mallinder, Ulster University law professor, talked about amnesty, and Andreé Murphy, Relatives for Justice Deputy Director, responded. Events also included, 'Survival and Resistance in the Occupied Palestinian Authority', 'Challenges of the Basque Political Peace Process', the annual Féile health lecture, plus panels on the 1967 Abortion Act and Irish language rights. And that's just a sample.

Féile needs an audience too. My contribution to this celebratory collection is as a grateful member of many audiences over the years. Some events are sure to gather a good crowd. West Belfast Talks Back is one; Scribes at the Rock is another. Then there are great one-off, overspill events, such as happened the year that St Thomas's assembly hall and upstairs room were packed to the rafters with people waiting to hear what Noam Chomsky had to say. He told us that he read the *Financial Times* every day because there's 'no better way to know what's happening in the world'. He talked about the global industrial-military complex and how we need to keep our eyes open to see its role in world affairs. His words were as timely and troubling in 1990 as they are today. He had facts at his fingertips. No notes. As I recall, he'd recently been reading some declassified US documents that revealed official alarm about the post-Second World War rise of new nationalism in Latin America with its radical philosophy that the beneficiaries of a country's resources should be its own people. The audience in St Thomas's was electrified. Did that US anxiety, about the spread of socialism near its southern border, contribute to the murder of Archbishop Óscar Romero in 1980? Answers were offered, and Chomsky's words were remembered when the author Matt Eisenbrandt spoke at a Féile 2017 event about 'The Assassination of a Saint' and the long struggle for justice through the US courts.

There are extraordinary highlights every year, local and international. Most people will have their own memories. *Binlids*, written by Christine Poland, Brenda Murphy, Danny Morrison and Jake Mac Siacais, was unforgettable. Produced and directed by Pam Brighton for the women's theatre company JustUs, it started with whispers rippling through the audience waiting for the play to start. 'Have you heard? They're bringing in internment again'. The effect was instant and shocking. A tremor of fear went through the crowd. For a moment, no more, people were plunged back to 1971 when the rumours were real. The audience couldn't have been better prepared for the vivid performance that followed. The cast, full of ingenious locals, played parts that revived outrageous, life-changing local events. Also dramatised, with a mix of anger and empathy, was the situation of some clueless squaddies shoved into the middle of a war. The tension was relieved at one point when someone watching was aroused to such a pitch that they shouted at an actor in a British Army officer uniform that he should take himself off and 'leave Ireland for good!' Whoops of laughter broke out. A Féile night to remember indeed.

It's called Féile An Phobail, the West Belfast Festival, or simply Féile. Whatever name you use, the summer gathering of people of all ages at play, in debate, telling stories, stretching their muscles, giving and receiving awards, capering to music and welcoming all comers in English, *as Gaeilge* and in translation, is a great gift and a global example of grit, creativity and fun. It is a collective act of resistance and reconciliation. You don't often see those words going together. They have been fused in Féile from the outset, when a beleaguered and maligned community decided to celebrate its own resources and invite others to join in and do the same.

From the beginning, Féile was an ingenious resistance to repression, division and warfare. It enabled local young people to convert pent-up frustrations into hard work, commitment and fun. Annual anti-internment protests around 9 August were transformed into a week-long opportunity for creativity and debate. Ex-prisoners, local justice activists and NGOs stepped up and made Féile happen. They still do. They took ownership of the space it offered to do things differently. The principle of reconciliation as a process of realising our collective dignity and building rights-based relationships between people and inside institutions, is the backbone of Féile. Huge numbers have always engaged and made efforts, great and small, to prompt self-empowering ways of voicing grievance, demanding justice, dealing with the past, recognising achievement and entertaining themselves. Critical to all of this has been the willingness of unionist and other political activists, academics, and religious and political leaders to join in. They've raised hard questions and expressed controversial views not shared by many in the audience. The sharp listening and exchange of witty repartee is legendary. All of this was (and is) done in the company of film buffs, actors, artists, comedians, playwrights and pop stars, to say nothing of street parties, fancy-dress parades and an annual protest against the use of plastic bullets. Transformative is not too strong a word to describe Féile.

Questions tackled elsewhere in this book are, how did it all start? And what keeps it going? There is some debate, as you would expect. You can read Ciarán de Baróid's account about Frank Cahill and Kate McManus along with some Quakers and others who organized the Upper Springfield Festival in 1973. When friends visited Frank in his last illness he gave them bright orange festival badges printed with 'The Upper Springfield Festival'. A kindness, a keepsake and a reminder not to forget. Other accounts of Féile's beginnings in 1988 are here too (see Deirdre McManus's and Jimmy 'Teapot' McMullan's).[3] There's truth in all the accounts. And there is no doubt that the seriousness and fun of Féile, like the Upper Springfield Festival before it, stems from the same source. It's both local and ancient; universal and new-fangled. It springs from the everyday solidarity, creativity and local leadership of people in dire circumstances who rely on each other first. It's as ancient as the Gaelic harvest festival of Lúnasa when, between the hard work of summer in the fields and bringing in the harvest, a halt was called to clan battles and local disputes. People gathered to celebrate the business of living. Féile provides a stage where past conflict is dramatised and dreams are realised (*Ballymurphy* and *A Night with George*, by Brenda Murphy); searing film captures prison struggle (*H3*, by Brian Campbell and Laurence McKeown); and redemptive song rings out loud and clear ('The Time Has Come', by Christy Moore). Where else would you find so many creative geniuses? The answer is easy: in any people's struggle, to articulate and claim their own worth and dignity, be it in Dublin's Ballymun or neglected housing estates in Cardiff, Glasgow and Liverpool. In these places and across the world, poverty and social injustice are crimes for which there is no accountability.

Let this reflection end with a breath of Black Mountain air and memories of Terry Enright taking us up the Mountain Loney and over the horizon. Terry, RIP, political and environmental activist and fit as a fiddle at the time, made the Black Mountain Walk an annual Féile event. On the way up, he'd stop at

---

[3] Kate and Deirdre McManus are my sisters.

viewpoints to chivvy slowcoaches (like me) and point out the beauty of the Belfast hills and the magnificent city below. Then, he'd bring us over to the great hole being gouged out of the side of the mountain by the quarry corporation. We'd stand, not too close, looking into the pit. Terry would talk, urging us to activism, and take off again, us in his wake. The craic was ninety and the day endless. A place that was once our Ballymurphy playground became, thanks to Terry, an education in resistance and a story of love for people and place. Go raibh maith agat.

Féile – politics and craic

JIM GIBNEY

I recall a short while before Féile an Phobail took to the West Belfast stage in 1988, as an embryonic people's festival, Gerry Adams said to me that he was keen to end the annual street disturbances which accompanied the anti-Internment protests, because of the threat to the lives of the protestors and in particular the young people involved in the protests and the street riots.

The British Crown forces were taking full advantage of young people expressing their anger about injustice on the streets, by firing salvos of plastic bullets at them, causing death in some cases, and grave injuries in many others. Criminal elements in the community also took advantage of the unrest and indulged themselves in a wrecking-spree of burnings and hijackings, causing the maximum disruption for people living under British military occupation in West Belfast. Gerry was keen that this annual chaos should end and be replaced with more positive activities that marked the Internment anniversary in a peaceful and reflective way.

Ironically enough, Féile an Phobail is the product — the response if you like — to two acts of violence. The decision by the unionist government of Brian Faulkner to use Internment, in August 1971, to quell the rising tide of nation- alist opposition to partition, and the post-1969 insurrection, and the violence of the British state which began when the SAS shot dead three IRA volunteers in Gibraltar in March 1988 and triggered off a series of events in Belfast which led to the IRA killing two British soldiers in Andersonstown in March 1988. It was the reaction to the deaths of the two soldiers which finally persuaded Gerry Adams to suggest the setting up of a people's festival during 'Internment Week', as a means of focusing people's energies in a positive way by showcasing the creative talents of the West Belfast community.

Following the deaths of the soldiers some politicians and elements of the media depicted the people of West Belfast as 'savages'. The response of the people to this demonisation was Féile an Phobail. Through Féile an Phobail, the People's Festival, the organisers were giving effect to Bobby Sands's hope that our revenge would be the laughter of our children. Because children and laughter play such a big part in Féile's activities. And what a response it was and has been annually for some thirty years. Féile's unique popular appeal from the outset was 'politics and craic' — fun and laughter and serious debate about current affairs. These two pillars remain the bed-rock on which Féile's clár has rested for three decades.

It is hard to be precise about when I joined the Féile's Debates and Discussions group, but it was probably 1989 or 1990. This is the main group which plans Féile's political debates and discussions. At the time, the leadership of Sinn Féin had appointed former Sinn Féin councillor and Mayor of Belfast, Tom Hartley, to lead its diplomatic engagement with the unionist and Protestant community and Tom had asked me to join him in these endeavours. In the course of these private discussions, it became clear that although unionists and nationalists lived on this island together, and had done so for some four hundred years, they did not share it as neighbours; indeed, they were strangers to each other in the land of their birth. This estrangement led to a centuries-old violent conflict.

It struck Tom that Féile could provide a platform for unionists to speak to the nationalist and republican people of West Belfast and vice versa. And so began an engagement between unionists, nationalists and republicans, in halls and on stages across West Belfast, at the height of the summer season in the midst of war, with all its human consequences. Out of these fledgling beginnings began a discourse between republicans and unionists that would develop in intensity and make a valuable and significant contribution to the IRA calling its ceasefire in August 1994.

This engagement has borne fruit on many occasions over the years especially in times of political crisis. From the outset, Féile followed an 'open door' policy. If you were part of the political problem, then you were part of the political solution, and participants were invited on that basis. The discussion and debates body, broadly speaking, reflected the political and community aspirations of its host community in West Belfast: democratic, republican, nationalist, socialist and feminist. But these aspirations did not get in the way of inviting people who did not share them. Indeed the Debates and Discussions group — D&D, as we christened ourselves — was keen to invite participants who did not share our views.

Back then it was fairly obvious that West Belfast and its people were not only being killed by the British Crown forces and their loyalist allies; they were also being demonised, marginalised, isolated and treated as a community that was not entitled to basic human and civil rights. Demonised by the media and marginalised by the political elites in Dublin, Belfast and London, the people of West Belfast were left to fend for themselves in their daily lives: economi-cally, socially and culturally. The reason for the demonisation and isolation was because the people of West Belfast supported the IRA and elected Gerry Adams as their MP, and many Sinn Féin councillors, including Alex Maskey, Sinn Féin's first councillor on Belfast City Council since 1920.

The West Belfast community had a long history of dealing with discrimina-tion and isolation. The unionist government at Stormont had, since partition in 1920, discriminated against the people of the area in terms of jobs, houses, cultural identity and inward investment. The community responded by using its own talents. Out of this spirit of self-help, self-assurance and self-confidence came the North's first Gaeltacht on the Shaw's Road; the rebuilding of Bombay Street, sacked by state and loyalist forces; the setting up of the *Andersonstown News*; the opening of a number of co-operatives; the formation of the Falls Taxi Association, and a strong and vibrant community and voluntary sector.

Féile's flagship events, such as the PJ McGrory Human Rights Lecture; West Belfast Talks Back and its youth equivalent; the Royal Health Lecture; an annual Shankill Road event; Palestinian and Basque Days and Tom Hartley's cemetery tours, along with many other events, were all opportunities to open our area up to the world beyond it. An important part of Féile's programme was also to open up West Belfast to the rest of Ireland, and artists like Bobby Ballagh and singer Christy Moore pioneered this as regular participants at Féile.

President Robinson's mould-breaking visit to West Belfast and her hand-shake with Gerry Adams, then the area's MP, helped pave the way for other important Féile participants, like President Mary McAleese and the late Taoi-seach Albert Reynolds.

The presence of well-known and respected people visiting Féile played a crucial part in ending the isolation and demonisation of the people of West Belfast and indeed of nationalists from across the North.

The human cost of the conflict is annually debated by Relatives for Justice and Coiste na nIarchimí, the republican ex-political prisoners' organisation. Former combatants — IRA activists, British soldiers and loyalists — shared platforms to speak about their experiences.

As Féile an Phobail approaches its 30th anniversary it has a new set of legs in terms of its management team; a new set of legs in terms of the new people who have joined the Debates and Discussions group. The energy and ideas from these important changes will ensure that Féile will prosper and continue in its role as a platform for new ideas, not just for the people of West Belfast but for all of the people of this island.

Féile – The real change-makers

JOBY FOX

I first heard the idea of a West Belfast Festival in 1987, while sitting in a London office run by then Celtic-rock band Energy Orchard. I was the bass player and Bap Kennedy was the singer. We were all from Andersonstown, living in London and we had just signed a major record contract. Our manager had mentioned that someone from Andersonstown had been in touch about us playing West Belfast's first festival, and he said he was finding it difficult to understand the accent. We all laughed!

I took it upon myself to contact a man who I was told was called Teapot. I laughed again as in true style there were no airs or graces about a name like that. I felt good about it already. I remember the call really well as I had been living in London for many years at that point and it was great to hear the voice of a 'no-frills' Belfast accent. It was the main man, Teapot! Teapot and I got on instantly and the way he put the whole idea about keeping the kids off the streets on 9 August was just hitting all my green lights. I was excited from the outset to get involved, although I was only one member of a six-piece band. I had to sell it to them also. Thankfully they all agreed to do a show.

We did the show in the front of the PD in Andersonstown and I remember the atmosphere was amazing — a feeling like everything was possible. I was so proud to be part of that. Two years later I was asked to join the committee. I worked alongside Tony Carlisle, Teapot and Hector, and the late Brendan Hughes aka 'The Dark'. It was odd, as I was a full year working with him and getting to know Brendan after I had just read the book *Ten Men Dead*, although at the time I didn't know it was the same guy I was reading about. I always found Brendan intelligent, smooth-talking and resourceful. I'm sure if it wasn't for the Troubles he could've chosen any career he wanted. I remember the first meeting I attended in the Andersonstown Leisure Centre. I spoke about community and the definition of community as I saw it — Protestant and Catholic and every other person here in West Belfast, the Shankill Road and all. I was pushing at an open door and everybody agreed on the definition. It was a couple of weeks later that listening devices were found in the room we had been meeting in. British intelligence were at their work. My God they didn't have anything better to do in those days.

Looking back, there are just so many unsung heroes — too many to mention, but Teapot, Hector, Brendan and Tony, those characters have influenced me in ways that they will never know. The fun and the laughter and the sheer determination that these guys showed, to drag Féile an Phobail into existence against the backdrop of mayhem that the Troubles brought to us, bore fruit time and time again for several generations. These guys and the likes of them are the real change-makers.

Film Festival – From West to Belfast-wide

Laurence McKeown

Many great ideas arise over a pint in the pub, or a glass of wine shared with friends over a meal. Madden's Bar was the setting for the inspiration that created the West Belfast Film Festival.

At the time, Brian Campbell and I had just started to write a screenplay for a film about the hunger strike, which eventually ended up as *H3*. I think it was a combination of that work, plus looking at the various genres of arts contained within Féile an Phobail, that turned our minds to the idea for a film festival — the only thing missing at that time from the Féile programme. In our view, rightly or wrongly, the reason for this absence was that the medium of film and filmmaking was still largely regarded at that time as the preserve of the elite or privileged, something outside the reach of working-class communities.

I didn't know anything about how to organise a film festival, so the following week I put an ad in the *Andersonstown News* asking if anyone out there *did* know. A relative of Áine O'Halloran, who worked for a Dublin festival at the time, spotted the ad and Áine contacted me. We met, the idea took shape, we had more discussions, and before long I was in the West Belfast offices of Barra McCrory, solicitor, to have him sign papers to establish the West Belfast Film Festival as a company.

Funding was a major issue of course. Féile itself was strapped for cash and had nothing to share with us. We had to seek out our own resources. Learning how to make an application to the City Council was another new adventure, though thankfully that's where the experience of those working with Féile really helped. Angela McCloskey in the Council offices was very helpful in processing our applications, though I imagine at the time she must have felt us fairly naive — though with huge ambitions! Some small businesses chipped in with sponsorship, which helped greatly, though it was a sign of the times when a certain business in the city centre gave us a few hundred pounds but asked that we not acknowledge it on any promotional materials; West Belfast, after all, was the 'terrorist community'. One man who was extremely helpful was Carl Von Ohsen of Making Belfast Work. From the moment we put our proposal to him and outlined what we hoped to achieve, he was totally on board and it was primarily due to his support and championing of the project that we got funding via his organisation.

There was only one possible venue for us in West Belfast: the cinema in the Kennedy Centre, which then consisted of one screen and no air-conditioning; nothing at all like today's multiplex venue. What we very quickly realised in our first year, however, was that given the very broad range of events that Féile already offered, and the fact that it took place in August, with fairly good weather, the last place people wanted to be during that week was inside a cinema. As a consequence, the following year we moved the film festival to its own slot later in the year. Whilst the film festival was started out as part of the Féile programme, we had our own separate identity, management structure, and volunteer staff. However, we shared the ethos of Féile — to bring arts to the people and people to the arts.

And artists supported us in doing just that. The opening film for the very first West Belfast Film Festival was *Land and Freedom*, directed by Ken Loach. The film, based on the Spanish Civil War, had not even been premiered at the time, but we were given permission to screen it as what is termed a 'sneak preview'. It was amazingly generous of Ken Loach. We had never been heard of before, had no track record, no funding, no staff, but I think that those may have been the factors that helped him make his decision.

Two other people who were very generous to us were Cathal Gaffney and Darragh O'Connell of Brown Bag Films Animation, Dublin, a company that had just been formed the previous year, 1994. Like us, Cathal and Darragh had huge ambitions but at the same time were firmly rooted in the community. For several years they travelled up to our festival on the train with their equipment and facilitated animation workshops for children during which the children made a short animated film that was then screened during the festival. The lads weren't even going to take their train fare from us. Today, Brown Bag Films is one of the world's most exciting, original and successful creative-led animation studios, with studio locations in Dublin, Toronto and Manchester and an office in LA. And fair play to them.

Central to the development of the film festival, was Michele Devlin. Michele tutored in media studies at Springvale Training Centre on the Springvale Road. I had met her through a mutual friend and once she heard of the project she was fully on board. Mary Lyons, CEO of Springvale Training, provided me with a desk in the centre, free of charge. Brian (Campbell) volunteered to handle the publicity for us at festival time and a number of other volunteers stepped in to help out. And that basically was the core team.

Gerry Adams always opened the festival for us and greeted guests. It was his support and promotion of the festival while in the US that prompted Martin Sheen to make a visit, which of course garnered huge publicity for us. Other very well-known actors who also appeared at the festival included Tom Berenger, Stephen Fry (whose shoe got stuck on a piece of chewing gum on the carpet in the cinema foyer) and Stephen Rea, amongst others. We always had an opening reception in the Patio restaurant, upstairs in the Kennedy Centre, thanks to the proprietors, Gerry and Rosetta, who were always willing to assist us in our efforts.

The film festival began to grow both in terms of audiences and in the number of days over which the programme stretched. The 1999 film festival was the most successful we had, but it also had negative consequences. It left the volunteer organisation drained and faced with two choices: we could revert back to being a small three or four-day festival or expand to become city-wide, with the potential to attract adequate funding and a core, salaried staff. After much soul-searching, we opted for the latter. There was no film festival in 2000 but in 2001 the West Belfast Film Festival was rebirthed as the Belfast Film Festival. Michele Devlin, in an amazingly generous and courageous move in terms of career, left her job as tutor in Springvale Training and became festival director.

There were no funds to pay her a salary or no office in which to place her; those followed later, largely due to her determination, skill, and persistence. Michele remains the director today, the festival has lovely offices in the city centre, has a permanent core staff, and it grows year on year. I remain on its board of management, am now also a member of the board of management of Northern Ireland Screen, and our collective goal now is to establish a purpose-built film centre in Belfast, similar to the Irish Film Centre in Dublin.

Since those early days, when the film festival kicked off, the film industry in the north of Ireland has snowballed. Having *Game of Thrones* (the most successful TV series in history) shot here has created huge publicity, but more crucially, has provided opportunities for a host of workers across a range of skills: actors, writers, producers, directors, makeup, set construction and many, many more. Some years ago, Marty McCann, one of the many young, emerging actors from the North, spoke at the launch of the Belfast Film Festival's programme. He told how, as a young boy growing up on the Falls Road, he would go along to the screenings at the West Belfast Film Festival, and how much that encouraged him to pursue an acting career. Whilst many other world-famous actors and directors have visited the Belfast Film Festival over the years, the comments from Marty, a local guy from the West, were validation for all we had sought to achieve.

In 2012, the film festival screened a number of films — crime dramas — in the High Court in Belfast. Barra McCrory, by then the new Director of Public Prosecutions, introduced the screenings and in his address recalled the day when I had walked into his office in West Belfast to get the company papers signed to establish the West Belfast Film Festival. Barra, the film festival, and all of us have come a long way since those days. From little acorns mighty oak trees grow. And they continue to blossom.

Féile – an uprising of community creativity, talent, pride, positivity and resistance

FERGUS Ó HÍR

'If I can't dance I don't want to be part of your revolution'. This famous quote from the eminent feminist and anarchist activist Emma Goldman could have served as a maxim for Féile an Phobail since its inception in 1988. For, despite the growing litany of horrors which had been inflicted on our community in the 20 years since our peaceful campaign for civil rights had been met with a violent response from the sectarian northern state, Féile had set us dancing.

At Féile we danced through long nights of Brush Shiels's magic up at Springhill. We did céilí dancing in the Cultúrlann. We danced to the soft pop music of Westlife and again we danced with the strutting rock music of Status Quo. At Féile we were warmed by the talent and integrity of Frances Black and Hot House Flowers, Kila, Damien Dempsey, Christy Moore and Robert Ballagh, and a host of other gifted and courageous performers and artists who helped bring some respite from the relentless brutality and repression beating down on our communities.

Féile was always about community. Every year, like blossoming flowers, our neighbours, our friends and people whom we only knew as nodding acquaintances in the street, metamorphosed before our eyes into singers, writers, musicians, actors, organisers, artists, and sports stars, or revealed other talents which we had never imagined they possessed. West Belfast, so often vilified and excoriated by a biased, servile and self-serving media, stepped out during the week of the Féile and showcased a depth and wealth of talent and creativity that often surprised even ourselves.

It is almost impossible, even for those of us who lived through it, to remember clearly the grim reality for many in Ireland, north and south, in the period leading up to when Féile was started. The bleak years of the 1980s were marked in the south by depressingly high levels of unemployment, as another generation of our young people were forced into emigration, leaving family, friends and communities, to seek a better life in foreign lands. In many rural areas, there weren't enough young people left to put a football team together. The unemployment exodus was joined by women with problem pregnancies, by gay people and by others trying to escape the often pulpit-driven social opprobrium and oppression of those dark times. Heated debates around the right to contraception and abortion were brought into riveting focus with the public pillorying of Joanne Hayes and her family during the infamous 'Kerry Babies' case and with the tragic death of 15-year-old Ann Lovett as she gave birth alone in a Marian grotto in County Longford. A grim period arising, according to writer Colm Tóibín, when 'an authoritarian church and a fragile insecure state combined to produce a sort of dark ages'.

In the North, after the seismic communal trauma and tragedy of the hunger strikes in the early 1980s, things were becoming bogged down in a grinding stalemate. It was difficult to imagine any movement forward. A vivid image of this period which stands out for me is of a sombre gathering late on a cold dismal night in March 1988 as people waited on Kennedy Way in Belfast for the bodies of three members of the local community, shot by the SAS in Gibraltar, to be brought back to their homes. As I observed the desolate scene, I remember the feeling that the situation in our community had reached a dark, depressing and dangerous low ebb. But things were quickly to spiral even lower. A murderous attack on the funeral of the three Gibraltar victims led to three more people being killed, and then two British soldiers, who drove into one of the subsequent funerals, were themselves killed. The British press and some of their politicians referred to the west Belfast community as a 'terrorist community'. Against this grim and brutal background, 'Féile an Phobail' was born. It represented an uprising of community creativity, talent, pride, positivity and resistance.

Many memories of the early Féile years are still vivid. I recall hearing the inspirational accordion player Tony McMahon from County Clare playing in a pub in Dublin. I took the opportunity to invite him to perform at a concert which some of us were organising in Conway Mill as part of Féile that year. He agreed to come and duly arrived in Belfast for the festival gig. As a famous, highly respected and talented guest we had given him top billing. But on discovering that our local fiddle playing genius Seán Maguire was also playing at the concert, Tony McMahon insisted that Seán be given top billing. No one, he said, should be placed higher on a concert billing that Seán Maguire. The situation was resolved with the two maestros performing together onstage to an enthralled audience. The character and calibre of Tony McMahon and his respect for the ethos of Féile was further demonstrated when he refused to take any payment for his performance.

Another of my memories of the early Féile days is of inviting the iconic, delightful and unique Cór Chúil Aodha from west Cork, along with Peadar Ó Riada, to play at a concert in Clonard Hall and to perform the Seán Ó Riada mass in Clonard Monastery. In those early 'make-it-up-as-you-go' days, after the concert, the choir, including the renowned vocalist Iarla Ó Lionáird, arrived back to the front room of my house, where they sang until the early hours of the morning while beds were sorted for those who wished to avail of them.

I have fond memories of our local songwriters and singers telling in their songs, with insightful and elegant fluency and humour, the stories of our struggle for justice here in Ireland, and the stories of other struggling oppressed peoples around the world. The brilliant cartoonist, singer and songwriter Brian Moore blossomed before our eyes into an accomplished playwright, under the lively direction of Pam Brighton and her Dubbeljoint Theatre Company. Pam similarly uncovered for us the thespian gifts possessed by that powerful singing talent Terry 'Cruncher' O' Neill. Others such as Gerry Jones, Bríd Keenan, Barry Kerr and a young McSherry family, often complemented by our exiles in Derry, Joe Mulheron and Eileen Webster, lit up concerts and singing sessions at Féile over the years with a passion and a beauty which simultaneously melted our hearts and steeled our resolve.

And of course Belfast's wonderful McPeake Family, often in company with the incomparable Seán Maguire, would enthral us with their stellar musical wizardry. While Seán Maguire and the McPeake Family were celebrated and honoured by traditional musicians around the world, they still worked diligently and resolutely without fanfare in the local community. Week after week through long years of wet winter evenings and fragile spring Saturday afternoons, they organised music classes in cold church halls and damp youth clubs, passing on the rich musical tradition to generations of young people. It is in no small measure due to them, and to some other local musical stalwarts, that Féile can always avail of a host of talented young local traditional musicians and that Belfast can now justifiably claim to be the foremost city for traditional music in Ireland.

But the importance of Féile an Phobail was not just the music and the craic. Of equal if not greater importance was that under the leadership of a series of dedicated, hardworking and able local Festival Directors, Féile brought a renewed sense of pride and confidence to a community which, for many years, had been demeaned, marginalised and brutalised for daring to stand up and demand basic civil and democratic rights. Also, by providing platforms for discussions and debates, by encouraging exchanges of views and perspectives, by creating opportunities to analyse lessons from our own situation and to learn from other struggles for justice throughout the world, Féile helped ensure that we were better able to understand how to advance the struggle for a just and equal society here in Ireland. The South African anti-apartheid leader Steve Biko famously wrote, 'the most potent weapon in the hands of the oppressor is the mind of the oppressed'. If, by providing platforms for alternative voices and different narratives, for new perspectives and informed discussions, Féile an Phobail has helped free some of our minds from the 'hands of the oppressor', we owe it a deep debt of gratitude.

Bringing colour, beaming children's faces and sunshine to the darkest of days

Caitríona Ruane

I was 24 years of age when I moved to West Belfast in March 1988 — the year Féile an Phobail was born. Before moving to Belfast, I had returned home to Ireland after working as a human rights worker in El Salvador, Nicaragua and Honduras. I then worked for a year in Trócaire's head office in Dublin. I lived in Clonard in a two-up, two-down house with an outside toilet. I had my showers for 50p in Whiterock or Beechmount Leisure Centres.

The week I moved to Belfast, Mairead Farrell, Dan McCann, and Seán Savage were killed by the SAS in Gibraltar. Six other people were killed in the days that followed. The two British Army corporals, David Howes and Derek Wood; Gillian Johnson in Fermanagh by the IRA; and Kevin Brady, Thomas McErlean and John Murray by Michael Stone. My abiding memory of that week is visiting wake houses and seeing families stunned with grief. The media reporting, apart from a few notable exceptions, was disgraceful and contributed to the ongoing demonisation of an entire community.

My father was dying of lung cancer at the time and I was back and forth to Mayo on a regular basis. It is only now, as I reflect back over 30 years later, that I realise how traumatised I was. Those were dark times and very dark days. True leadership and real political vision were needed.

Féile an Phobail, the People's Festival, was one of the most important initiatives to come out of West Belfast. It was founded to challenge the establishment's systematic demonisation of the community. It was a community-led showcase of all that was good and creative about West Belfast. It was supported by artists, playwrights and authors, throughout Ireland and internationally who were not afraid to stand up and be counted. Brave people. It is worth remembering that at this time the Birmingham Six and Guildford Four were still in jail and Special Branch was raiding homes of affluent Booterstown parishioners who were protesting for their release. Special Branch used to stand outside RTÉ studios as the audience were going in to make sure no member of Sinn Féin or their 'fellow travellers' slipped through and 'broke' the Section 31 censorship law.

I remember the first Féile, the parade, the 'I love West Belfast' stickers, Croí na Féile, the mural judging competition by Robert Ballagh. (If my memory serves me correctly the mural of Nelson Mandela won — he was also still in jail). Most of all I remember the street party in Benares Street where I lived. Each end was closed off to cars, bunting was put up, chairs and tables were put out on the road, music played and every single person in that street came out and joined the party. In my memory, the sun shone but didn't it always when we were young? The beauty of Féile was that any organisation in West Belfast could organise events and they would be included in the programme. The organisation I helped to co-found, the Centre for Research and Documentation (CRD), organised events every year for Féile — a film festival, international photojournalist exhibition, international speakers etc. Féile grew and grew and became so big and so successful and most importantly so loved by the community that funders found it increasingly difficult to ignore.

I applied for the post of Director of Féile in November 1996. Funding for CRD had dried up, I had just had my second child, and I began working in January the following year. Féile's office was on the top floor of the old Cultúrlann. Three months later we moved into Teach na Féile on the Falls Road, which was opened by Albert Reynolds and Gerry Adams. This was not an easy project to work in, because there were such high expectations of Féile. Everyone in the community had opinions on what Féile should or should not be doing and they were not shy about voicing those views. For anyone who worked in Féile, their social life changed forever. No more could you go out for a quiet drink. The Féile team carried out a very thorough and honest community consultation and published it. We did a further independent study to show how much Féile was contributing economically to the local community. This was aimed at funders, many of whom were still openly discriminating against the festival.

Over the next five years, Féile grew alongside the peace process. A new children's festival, *Draíocht*, was founded with top quality arts for children of all ages. One of my childhood favourites, Wanderly Wanderly Wagon, came up from Dublin and performed their world-class puppet show. On Saturday night, my six brothers and sisters and I used to watch them on RTÉ while we had banana sandwiches for our tea. It was a lovely moment for me to see the Lambert Theatre Company performing live for children in West Belfast. We had a vibrant Arts and Disability programme, a radio station that got a licence twice a year. The Irish-language community were the Croí na Féile and in Culturlann during Féile week locals mixed with world-famous artists, writers and politicians.

Bringing colour to the darkest of days: *Caitríona Ruane*

Féile worked with our sister festivals throughout the city: Lower Ormeau, Ardoyne Fleadh, New Lodge, Bawnmore and others. We jointly organised the first ever St Patrick's Carnival in Belfast and brought tens of thousands of people into the city. The peace process was in its infancy and Féile played an important role in building small but important links with the unionist and loyalist communities. We loaned our street puppets to Shankill and Suffolk festivals. Shankill Women's Centre had a weekly slot on the radio and presented their programme from Teach na Féile. UUP Mayor, Bob Stoker, launched the Film Festival with Gerry Adams. Michael McGimpsey, the then Minister for Arts, joined President Mary McAleese and Gerry Adams in Clonard Monastery with the Ulster Orchestra and the wonderful Sky's the Limit Theatre company performing to a full house.

Féile an Phobail is an amazing organisation. It has achieved so much against all the odds and during very difficult and dangerous times. People often ask me for my favourite moment or particularly special memories. I could not pick one, there were too many. The Afro-Cuban All-Stars performing in the marquee and over a thousand people chanting 'No al bloqueo', 'No to the blockade'; the Mexican Mariachi band pouring their heart out on the streets of West Belfast; people queuing for their bin lids and *Just a Prisoner's Wife* tickets; the dignified, ground-breaking LGB&T event in Cultúrlann; Tommy Tiernan in the radio station at 1am after his gig; the International Food Fayre, packed to the rafters with people queuing up for their 50p portions; Christy Moore; Frances and Mary Black; Samantha Mumba; Westlife; the inimitable Shane MacGowan; and Kilfenora Céilí Band … you name it, Féile had it.

All those and many more wonderful memories flood my mind. But none of them can compare to the faces of the children as they walked in the carnival parade, in costumes that they made with local artists, in local community centres. Their faces said it all. For these children, armed British soldiers in their streets had become the norm. Ugly military barracks dominated West Belfast, from Poleglass to Divis. Dark green and grey were the colours of the conflict. What Féile an Phobail did was bring colour to those children's lives, colours in all their glory — reds, yellows, pinks, blues, oranges, purples, and one hundred shades of green … and of course sunshine.

Breithlá shona duit Féile an Phobail, may you have many more of them.

I thank Féile for the days

MÁIRTÍN FLYNN

Roads melted, reservoirs emptied and ginger people hid indoors throughout the long hot summer of 1995. By then, Féile an Phobail was a firm fixture in West Belfast life and you'd have struggled to find someone who wasn't feeling the buzz as August approached.

I spent part of that summer heaving staging around a range of venues with my cousin Annette and her husband Paul. They were both heavily involved in dramatic arts and were helping bring Féile drama performances to life. At that time, the work of people like Marie Jones and Pam Brighton was making serious waves on the thespian scene and productions that premiered here were ending up on Broadway (no, not that Broadway, the New York one) and London's West End.

In photographs from 1988, I'm pictured in St James's plastered in 'I Love West Belfast' stickers, enjoying the very first Féile fun day, held in the vortex of one of the darkest years of our conflict. By the ceasefire year of 1994, I'd already popped my Springhill cherry, boogieing away at the dance night as a teenage raver. But 1995 was the first year I'd helped out and I loved it. Getting a jook behind the scenes made me want to do more.

Féile was outstanding that year — I even dressed up as an Orangeman as part of the community parade, with a pack of loonies from Beechmount. I'm sure this was the first year the comedy nights took place at the Dairy Farm — Michael Smiley headlined and at that time he was famous for Smiley's People on Channel 4's Naked City. The next year I asked our Annette to ask if there was any extra help needed.

Féile's offices at that time were upstairs in the Cultúrlann, and I shuffled across one sunny morning, only to find nobody really knew what to do with me. Ever resourceful, Chrissie Mhic Siacais scribbled a note, handed it to me and packed me off to Springvale Training Centre, where I soon found Triple FM — Féile's very own radio station — had begun broadcasting that very day. 'Ask for

Mart or Mal', ordered Chrissie, and when I found them, I couldn't possibly have imagined what lay ahead — that day changed my entire life.

I got tore in as Mart barked the orders to the volunteers and Mal barked 'rock and roll' at every opportunity. It was anarchic, mental, hilarious, compelling and incredibly enjoyable and some of us worked there day and night for four weeks, answering phones, doing the sound desk, facilitating live bands and making endless amounts of tea as we were fed for free every night by local take-away outlets.

Conflict still loomed large, and that summer was one of the 'Bad Drum-crees'. There was no IRA ceasefire and there were also high tensions around the Torrens area in North Belfast, something our Ardoyne colleagues were quick to point out to us peacenik 'Westies'. I soon joined the radio station committee, working with Veronica Brown, and I led the advertising team, which helped keep the station afloat.

Ciaran Quinn roped me onto the management committee of the Féile itself in late 1997 and I worked with the staff through my time at university, both in the radio station and at events. I benefited from professional coaching from journalists, most notably Anne Cadwallader.

The Féile spread its wings at this time, beyond summertime, and Féile an Earraigh was born, with the St Patrick's Day festivities and carnival now main-streamed into Belfast City Council's annual events. I soon secured a PR job in the BBC (thanks to a reference from then Féile Director, Caitríona Ruane) and I've since worked in a range of public-sector, third-sector and regeneration organisations, working with the media and getting good stories out to the wider public. I've met and worked with Hollywood A-listers like Obi Wan Kenobi himself, Ewan McGregor, and supermodels like Naomi Campbell, and I'm on first-name terms with cast members from Eastenders. But I also stood in the Falls Park one sunny day chatting to another Hollywood actor, Tom Berenger, at the Féile Fun Day, and I got a swift nod off the head on another occasion from President Jed Bartlet from the West Wing — sometimes known as Martin Sheen, as Michele Devlin swished him round the Falls for our film festival. I remember Stephen Fry's biopic of Oscar Wilde premiered in the Kennedy Centre and Fry sitting on The Kelly Show saying his ma would have been horrified at him travelling into areas like Divis just a few years before, as the only thing you ever saw about this place in England were riots — we were in changing days.

The cinematic aspect of Féile's work is another which grew wings and took off on its own, under Michele Devlin and Lorney McKeown's direction. It soon blossomed into the Belfast Film Festival, a staple on the city scene to this day. Féile an Phobail broadened our horizons and brought the world to our doorstep. Take a look at the Féile alumni — you'll see them on TV, others run their own festivals now and more again are excelling in their careers in a range of roles, leaving deep impacts in their very own way.

Féile showed our young people that all we had to do was reach out and grab the world. I thank everyone I came across during my 'Féile Years' and I still attend events every August. My kids now attend too — the next generation is already feeling the benefit of Ireland's biggest community festival as it heads happily towards its third decade.

I thank Féile for the days.

Irish, queer and equal?

CLAIRE HACKETT

The first debate on gay issues in Féile took place in 2000. It was headlined 'Irish Queer and Equal?' and took place in An Chultúrlann, with a panel of four speakers from Ireland and the USA. Gerry Adams came to open the debate and stayed on as a member of the panel. The speeches were eloquent and passionate, the room was packed with gay and straight people and the atmosphere was electric. It felt like a historic occasion and it remains one of the things I am most proud of having been involved in.

It's hard to remember now just how oppressive the atmosphere of homophobia was back then. It was commonplace for public figures, particularly in the churches and unionism, to talk about sinfulness and perversion. It was a very toxic environment for young people to come out as gay, bi-sexual, lesbian or transgender. It was because of this that a feminist group I was involved in, called Clár na mBan, decided to organise a talk as part of Féile, which by this time had a reputation for ground-breaking discussion. Clár na mBan had been most active in the previous decade, when we campaigned around women's involvement in the peace process and most memorably organised a conference called Women's Agenda for Peace in March 1994. By 2000, Clár na mBan was no longer very active, but a few of us — Marie Quiery, Oonagh Marron and I — decided to organise the 'Irish, Queer and Equal?' debate.

My memory is that we began with the idea of debating the banning of gay organisations from the St Patrick's Day parades in New York and Boston. This seemed a good way of questioning what a queer identity meant in an Irish context. This discussion led us to working with another group, Peace Watch Ireland, a US activist organisation doing solidarity work in the north of Ireland with communities from the Ormeau Road and Garvaghy Road affected by Orange marches. Several of that group were gay and lesbian and had a history of activism in different struggles in the US. We discussed the topic of the talk with Peace Watch and finally came up with the title 'Irish, Queer and Equal?' This was taken from a protest slogan — 'Irish and Equal' — that was current at the time and asserted the struggle for equality of Irish identity.

Our speakers were Joan Garner, Sean Cahill and Clarence Patton from Peace Watch, all of whom were community activists in social justice movements in Boston, New York and Washington, and also Kieran Rose from the Gay and Lesbian Equality Network based in Dublin. The chair was Marie Mulholland, a former member of Clár na mBan, who was by then working for the newly established Equality Authority in the South.

We recorded the event and transcribed it in a report (which anyone interested can get from the Féile office, which still has a box of them). I was in charge of recording the debate as I had by then started work on Falls Community Council's oral history archive, Dúchas. It really dates the period to say that I was using a minidisk recorder — then the newest form of digital recording, but now obsolete. The minidisk lasted 75 minutes before it had to be changed and I can remember sitting in the audience trying to remember when I would have to walk up to the front table where I had placed the recorder, in order to change the disk. In the event I misjudged and lost about 15 minutes of discussion. This was at the point in the debate when Gerry Adams was being challenged about his participation in the St Patrick's Day march in New York, which banned the participation of ILGO — Irish Gay and Lesbian Organisation — so when we launched the subsequent report there was some suspicion about the missing section, but I knew that it was my mistake rather than censorship.

Gerry did come in for some criticism from members of the audience, but as organisers I can remember that we were really pleased that he had agreed to our request to open up the debate as he was very much in demand during Féile. His presence was important to us as a gesture of solidarity with the very marginalised community we then were. So we were even more pleased when we realised that he was going to stay for the whole event, having been drawn into the discussion. I can also remember clearly the exhilaration I felt at seeing the room fill up with community activists from West Belfast, who came to support the event, as well as with gay and lesbian activists from across the city and other parts of Ireland, many of whom had never been to Féile before. The report records that over two hundred people attended what was said to be one of the largest, liveliest and most diverse discussions in Féile that year.

When I read the 'Irish, Queer and Equal?' report again I can see that while there was talk about legislating for equality in employment and services there was no mention at all of partnership or equal marriage. It's an amazing thought now, when marriage equality has become symbolic of lesbian and gay rights in general. The speakers did set a very strong context of discussing LGBT oppression within other forms of social justice struggle — class, race and gender equality. The subsequent debate reflected this and there was a lot of discussion about building alliances and linking struggles. As I read the report again I feel the power and continuing relevance of this discussion about intersectionality. And I am reminded why the Féile debate and discussion programme matters so much.

Éacht phobail – ceiliúradh pobail

JAKE MAC SIACAIS

Cá dtosaíonn tú le scéal Fhéile an Phobail? Chuir mé an cheist sin orm féin nuair a iarradh orm an píosa beag seo a scríobh. Ar ndóigh, níl ach aon fhreagra amháin ann agus sin é go dtosaíonn tú leis an phobal féin. Bhí na céadtaí bainte leis an Fhéile ón tús, iad uilig i mo thuairim chomh tábhachtach lena chéile. Bígí cinnte nach bhfuil mé chun titim isteach sa tseanmheancóg agus liosta a lua — nó is cinnte go bhfágfainn daoine amach — agus cé go ndeir siad uilig nach mbaineann obair phobail le daoine aonair, an uair a fhágann tú daoine 'tábhachtacha' amach ní fada go bhfaighidh tú moll mór gearán.

Chaith mise mo chéad fhéile i gcomhluadar beirt Bhascach ag ól fíon úill mar ba nós liom. Bhí an triúr againn, agus daoine eile ina sealanna, buailte in éadan balla an ollphobail a bhí ardaithe (más ar éigin a bhí sé) ar na páirceanna ag an Nasc Theas, nó 'Chalky Field' mar a thugtaí air. Ní fhaca mé duine de na Bascaigh chéanna go ceann fiche bliain, go dtí go raibh mé ag cóisir teacht abhaile dó in Iruna, in Euskal Herria, nuair a scaoileadh saor ó charcair Spáinneach é, áit ar chaith sé an seal fada idir an dá bhabhta drabhláis céanna.

Fanfaidh oíche an ollphobail sin go fada i mo chuimhne — oíche den scoth a bhí ann: Brush Shiels, buanchara na Féile, Energy Orchard agus an Century Steel Band, a bheadh go minic ag Springhill ina dhaidh sin, a bhí ar an ardán. Bhí an ceol go híontach cé gurbh fhearr i bhfad an chraic, an damhsa gan srian, agus an comhspiorad a bhí ann sa scaifte iontach a phlódaigh isteach ainneoin na fearthainne amuigh agus más buan mo chuimhne an fhearthainn istigh chomh maith. Bhíomar saor (fiú mura mbeadh sé ach ar feadh tamaill), in ard spioraid agus in áit eile ar fad ón slad agus ón chaillteanas a bhí ag titim amach thart orainn sa bhliain uafásach sin de 1988.

Is deacair creidbheáil anois, ach idir Mí Eanáir agus seachtain na Féile 1988, cailleadh seasca agus a sé duine sa choimhlint anseo. Mharaigh Óglaigh na hÉireann (ÓNH) 32 ball d'Fhórsaí na Corónach. Maraíodh beirt shibhialtach ag ÓNH de bharr iad a bheith ina dtogálaithe ar bheairic Arm na Breataine agus mharaigh ÓNH, freisin, ball den UVF a bhí, dar leo, ina ghunnadóir dílseach. Maraíodh 17 sibhialtaigh Caitliceacha neamhchiontacha, 15 acu ag buíonta báis dílseacha. Fuair an bheirt eile bás i dtaisme buamála ar Bhóthar na bhFál, ag lámha ÓNH. Maraíodh ceathrar sibhialtach Protastúnach ag lámha ÓNH, triúr de thaisme, máthar, athar agus mac a chailleadh i mbuama a bhí dírithe ar Bhreitheamh Árd Cúirte, agus maraíodh Protastúnach neamhchiontach eile 'de thaisme'. Chaill ÓNH naonúr dá mball féin, ceann sa Saorstát ag lámha an Gharda Síochána agus duine eile a scaoil siad féin a rá gur brathadóir a bhí ann.

Bhí aithne phearsanta agam ar sheachtar de na hóglaigh sin agus chaith mé seal i bpriosún le ceathrar acu. Duine amháin, Kevy McCracken, a bhí ina chara cillín agam ar an pluid. Bliain dhorcha, phianmhar í 1988 agus an bliain inár thug státrúnaí Shasana 'the terrorist community' agus 'savages' ar mhuintir Iarthar Bhéal Feirste, rud a chuir go mór leis na hiarrachtaí a bhí ar bun le féile a chur ar siúl, a thabharfadh ardán dearfach do phobal íontach an cheantair seo agus a chuirfeadh bolscaireacht na bunaíochta ó mhaith.

Bhí Féile an Phobail ag lonrú gathanna dóchais agus gathanna solais a réab fríd an dorchadas a bhí inár dtimpeall. Bhí ardán ann i gcónaí do thallann úr agus ba dheacair gan moladh a thabhairt do na laochra a sheas le pobal s'againn nuair a bhí gach duine eile dár gcáineadh. Bhí an féile oscailte do chách agus rinneadh iarracht ón tús an lámh a shíneadh amach chuig pobail eile agus chun cinntiú go gcluinfear guthanna éagsúla ag plé mórcheisteanna reatha.

Bhí baint agam féin le Coiste na nDíospóireachtaí agus le go leor eile, ina measc an Poc Fada, a bhí á reáchtáil ag Ger Rogan agus ag Eamonn Mór Ó Faogáin, nach maireann, é ag tabhairt cupla punt isteach do Ghaelscoileanna gan mhaoiniú. Bhí clár léirmheasta nuachtáin agam féin agus ag Danny Morrison ar Raidió na Féile. Bhí an Raidió an-tábhachtac ar fad ó thaobh an pobal a lárnú san Fhéile agus é faoi stiúir Mart Holland, duine de na daoine is cruthaithí agus is gealgháirí a d'fhéadfá a fháil. Ní thiocfadh liom gan Springhill a lua, píosa talaimh caite clochach, timpeallaithe le sconsa, ach é plódaithe achan oíche le dubhscaifte a bhí ann do chuid de na coirmeacha ceoil ab fhearr a bhí san Iarthar le fada, fada an lá. Ní dhéanfaidh mé dearmad go deo ar 'iompar amach' Shane MacGowan, a tháinig chuig teach s'againn cupla uair maith sula dtáinig An Dark Hughes agus Pat Beag McGeown le Shane féin, a bhí siad i ndiaidh cailleadh ag an aerfort. Laoch a bhí i Shane ag m'iníon is sinne ach d'imigh sin nuair a tháinig sí ar sa chistin s'againn, é stiúctha gan bhróg nó stoc mar a deir an seanamhrán. Bhí a fhios ag muintir an Iarthair ariamh go mbíonn cosa cré ag gach laoch ach bhí an chré idir coismhéara Shane i bhfad barraíocht do m'iníon bhocht. Sin ráite, thug sé coirm cheoil den scoth dúinn an oíche chéanna, ainneoin an gin agus an martini.

D'fhan mé gníomhach i bhFéile an Phobail ar feadh na mblianta ach sna mall nóchaidí d'éirigh mé as aon ról a imirt. Bhí, ar ndóigh, proifisiúnú a dhíth ar an Fhéile, dá mba rud é go raibh sé le bheith inmharthanach san fhadtréimhse, ach bhí i bhfad barraíocht difríochtaí agam le stíl, éiteas, agus bunpholaitíocht úr a tháinig chun cinn agus b'éigean domh cinneadh drogallach a ghlacadh gan bheith gníomhach a thuilleadh. Caitheamh i bhfad barraíocht babaithe amach le huisce an fholcadáin le linn na tréimhse sin.

Ach tá Féile an Phobail i bhfad níos mó ná aon duine aonair agus tá ceiliúradh tríocha bliain buailte linn. Go raibh rath ar an fhéile sna tríocha bliain atá romhainn, go dté sé ó neart go neart agus go raibh sé ann nuair atá lucht a bhunaithe i bhfad ar shiúl. Go bhfana an pobal ag croílár na Féile go deo, mar gan an pobal níl ann d'aon fhéile i ndáiríre.

Moving mountains and meadows

Terry Goldsmith

It was at one of our regular sit-downs with Gerry Adams and Aidan McAteer that Aidan Crean and I were introduced to the idea of the Féile. The meetings were weekly at that time, as we pushed our ambitions for a Bog Meadows Nature Reserve. Gerry, Aidan and Siobhán O'Hanlon used these meetings to help smooth the edges of our naive plans and strategies to win support for our objectives. Aidan C. had a very strong knowledge of birds and their behaviours. I loved spending time in the countryside and had an appreciation of wild land-scapes. Neither of us had any experience of campaigning or politics. What we had in abundance was enthusiasm and they helped to point that in the right directions. They made introductions to people like Fr Des Wilson, Tom Hartley, Terry Enright, Máirtín O'Muilleoir and other local community campaigners. Environmental conservation was very low on most peoples' agendas in those days and we were very pleasantly surprised by the genuine interest shown in our project. You have to remember that back in the mid 1980s 'saving biodiversity' still meant putting your whites in with your dark wash.

Aidan Mac introduced the topic of the August commemorations by asking for our views on bonfires. Aidan Crean sneered. I knew he hated bonfires — despite the fact that he had been a bit of a firebug himself as a youngster. All we could see now was the damage they created through the toxic fumes they spewed out into the air. We also hated the mess they created before, during and after the event and the fact that trees would be hacked down to supplement the tyres, mattresses, old suites, furniture, rolls of roof felt, discarded doors and just about anything else the kids could get their hands on that would ignite. I knew the list well — I had collected for the August bonfires too. We both knew we sounded like hypocritical killjoys but we couldn't hide our dislike for bonfires. Gerry Adams's ears pricked up when we mentioned trees being cut down. 'Really?' he said looking at Aidan Mac. Aidan affirmed our assertion. Gerry had obviously had better things to do than collect wood for bonies in his youth.

He told us that there had been a proposal to change the way the community marked the anniversary of the introduction of internment and part of that was to move away from bonfires. We supported that. They then trotted out the proposals for a new community festival and asked if we would play a part. Of course we would.

As we discussed the role we could play in the festival, I must have switched off. I was probably thinking about all the ideas they had mentioned about other activities and was making a mental note of all the offerings I wanted to attend. Concerts, talks, cemetery tours, displays, exhibitions and more were mentioned. My mind was whizzing through all the options and I mustn't have been concentrating on what was being discussed as our contribution. I vaguely remember mentions of a Bog Meadows tour, a talk to outline our proposals for the Bog Meadows Reserve and even, at one point, a mention of an historian being brought in to talk about the industrial heritage of Milltown Glen. One way or another, I have absolutely no recollection of having volunteered to take part in the opening parade.

A few weeks after that meeting a group of environmental campaigners had agreed to gather a band of supporters and groups of kids to add a splash of colour to the parade. I agreed to that and made my way up that day to the Busy Bee, where we had arranged to meet up. I hadn't given it any thought at all. There were plenty of parades started or ending at the Busy Bee. Nothing new there. I arrived with my two arms the same length, with no particular agenda. I was a bit bemused to see Gerard Daye standing wearing some kind of costume and holding a big mouse's head under his arm. His face was like a wet weekend. Everyone else was buzzing around trying to organise kids who were also dressed up or had their faces painted. As I was looking for my steward's armband I heard someone mention 'woodland creatures'. I was just thinking what a great theme that was when I felt a ball of slightly damp and musty furriness being thrust into my arms. 'There you go, comrade.' It was Terry Enright and he rushed off saying something about heading up Shaw's Road towards the quarry. 'What do you want me to do with this?' I shouted after him. He didn't reply. I turned to Aidan Crean, who had just arrived with a large group of family, friends and their brightly attired children. "Who is this for', I asked? 'Don't start', he replied. 'You agreed to do this.' '*What?*' I responded. 'What even is it?' 'It's a rabbit', he replied. 'The head is in the boot of one of those cars. Hurry up we're late.' He was obviously taking great delight from my discomfort. I should explain at this point that I was very much a shirt-and-tie young man. I was comfortable at meetings and conferences. I didn't climb up ladders with posters and I didn't do dressing up as a rabbit to walk down the main road where people could know me. I pointed out that this costume was blue and therefore not a proper representation of our local rabbit population — most of whom are brown. No-one was having it.

And so it was that my introduction to this fantastic community festival was dressed in a washed-out blue rabbit costume that absolutely stank of the sweat of a previous wearer. We headed down towards Dunville Park carrying a massive 'Save the Black Mountain' sign, waving at people along the route. I was grateful that at least the smelly head protected my identity and maintained my bruised dignity. I suppose, if I am honest, as we went along, I sort of grew into the role a bit and in no time at all was hopping along waving like a March hare, carried away by the enthusiasm of the crowds. Given the explosion in the popularity of the Féile in subsequent years, it is nice to remember being a part of it all the way back then — even if uncomfortably incognito.

I remember that same year attending the annual Ardoyne guider race along Brompton Park. There was a massive crowd in attendance and the atmosphere was electric. The guiders were hurtling down the relatively gentle slope while the madmen who occupied them threw missiles at each other and tried to ram their opponents off the road, over the kribby and into the assembled masses on the footpath. There was quite a buzz along the route as Gerry Adams and Martin McGuinness arrived to witness the spectacle. Spotting me walking by, Adams called me over and said how great it would be to have something like this organised to travel down the Mountain Loney at Newhill the following year. In an instant I realised that besides climbing ladders and dressing as blue rabbits that speeding down the side of a mountain in a home-made go cart was another thing I didn't do. I just smiled politely and suggested that I would push if he drove. The offer was never followed up.

In the years since there have been many Féile highlights for me. I remember waiting (for a long time) for Shane MacGowan and the Pogues to come on stage at Beechmount Leisure Centre. I got talking to the groups of people on either side of me and was surprised and delighted when both groups quietly admitted to being from two areas of South Belfast that would not have normally been associated with the Féile. Two groups of people from unionist areas attending a community festival concert on the Falls Road would have been unheard of in years before. I could see then that the hopes of the founders really were coming to fruition — an inclusive celebration, open to all.

Following on from our early campaign, The Bog Meadows has been designated an official local nature reserve. Ulster Wildlife took over that wild oasis and oversaw the project. New paths have been introduced to open up access to the community. An area at the southern end of the reserve has been retained for nature conservation, with grown-over ponds re-opened and cattle brought in to reduce the length of the grass and allow plants to flourish. Friends of the Bog

Meadows continue to work in the area and have maintained a constant effort on the bird-ringing programme, to help monitor the health of the wildlife. There is still a lot to do to transform what we have achieved so far into what we dreamt of at that time.

On Black Mountain, The National Trust has helped to realise the dreams of our late friend, Terry Enright, by acquiring and opening up Black Mountain and Divis. On the back of their success at the Bog Meadows, Ulster Wildlife acquired a new reserve at Slievenacloy. The gaping hole of the massive quarry operation, which we campaigned so much against, has changed a lot. The process of filling in the vast chasms extracted from the mountain over many years has begun but will be a long-term project. The Belfast Hills Partnership has developed from those early campaigns and it is our hope to eventually open an access route the whole way across the hills — in line with our ambitions of 30 years ago. At a recent meeting, it was notable that three of Terry's sons, Liam, Niall and Feargal, were all in attendance and each made significant contributions to the proceedings. The legacy of our campaigns continues.

Against this evolving backdrop, we have continued to be involved with the Féile. The Meadows to Mountains walks developed from the Belfast Hills walks in recent years and have attracted good numbers of people from across Belfast and beyond. I have been proud to have continued that association along with my fellow long-term campaigner Aidan Crean, and working alongside campaigners from the Cairde Páirc na bhFál. One of the major lessons we took from those early meetings was the importance of looking beyond your own project or campaign. I was very aware of that as we sat down with people like Micheál Brennan, Micky Culbert Jnr and Deborah McLaughlin to help organise these walks.

The Féile itself is unrecognisable from that first attempt by local leaders to galvanise the vibrant soul of a downtrodden but resourceful community. What was a commemoration of oppression has become a celebration of our culture and resolve. I have watched from the side-lines as a new professionalism has transformed it into a massive community festival — comparable with the best in Europe. I have witnessed my daughters participate in the opening parade dressed as fish and nowadays my granddaughters have taken up that mantle and look forward to the annual celebrations.

If we can do it, so can you

CHRISTINE POLAND

My experience of Féile was so much fun — I made the best of friends and I learnt so much. I was involved at different levels, volunteering from the start, and then during the second decade I spent five years on the management committee, followed by over four years employed as the training coordinator. These roles provided massively different experiences and perspectives.

It's still hard to believe that 30 years have passed. I remember my kids going to workshops and coming home delighted with life at the stuff they'd created — recordings of animations, jewellery, lanterns, animals, painted glasses, candles, (unidentifiable) pottery, ceramics, photographs — you name it, my house is full of it; Féile played a significant part in their childhoods.

I loved the kids' concerts: seeing their faces when the likes of Samantha Mumba, Girls Aloud or Westlife (to name a few) came on stage was priceless — I nearly fainted myself for God's sake. The international night was one of the biggest in Féile. I remember when it was only Chrissie Mhic Siacais and I doing the bar with 12 Basque nationalists upstairs in Cultúrlann. From there to the marquee with backdrops designed and installed by the BBC was impressive.

Margaret McKernan made a giant backdrop, black with white lettering that said Féile an Phobail; it covered the whole back wall of the stage. I never ceased to be so proud when I saw artists like The Proclaimers, Altan, Alabama 3, Afro Celt Sound System, the Harlem Gospel Choir, Mary Black, Frances Black, Ardal O'Hanlon and Dara Ó Briain to name a few, perform in front of that backdrop.

One of my favourite memories of all time was working in the marquee down Kennedy Way one Saturday afternoon. The Ulster Orchestra was on stage dressed in their finest, with our backdrop behind them. Out front, the audience were casually wearing shorts and sandals (Ciaran Quinn) and young children were doing tumbles on the ground; it was brilliant, etched in my brain forever.

These are but a few examples of a million experiences that made Féile more than just fun; it was inspirational and educational, and to us Féile wasn't just a job, but a way of life. I couldn't write about Féile without talking about JustUs theatre company, how it was born and where it brought us as a group.

Chrissie Mhic Siacais is my mate and was the development worker with Féile. She'd been tasked with running an event for International Women's Day and came up with the idea of a play. She asked me to go to a planning meeting with her, but I didn't really want to go. I left that meeting with a part in the play and I'd to write it myself, so did Bridie, Sue, Maureen, Annemarie, the two Mairéads, Geraldine, Maura, Niamh and later Donna. Chrissie was the producer and Margaret Mooney stage manager. Siobhán was with us from then too. This would become our first play, *Just a Prisoner's Wife*.

Some of the actresses were actually living that life, with husbands still in prison. Some had travelled to English prisons and experienced all the hardship that went along with that. We told their stories and many others in the play. Though planned as a one-off show, we toured *Just a Prisoner's Wife* on and off for nearly 20 years.

For us, the most momentous performances were with republican prisoners both in Portlaoise gaol and the H-Blocks, which happened not long before those prisoners were released under the Good Friday Agreement. We couldn't believe we got permission to perform in the jails, and not only did we go into them, but on both occasions we were given free access to perform the play and then socialise on the wings with the prisoners. This was unprecedented.

Pam Brighton directed the play. Pam, Marie Jones and Mark Lambert formed Dubbeljoint Theatre Company in 1991 and premiered several of their plays during Féile, including the famous *Night in November* about a Northern Ireland football fan having an epiphany during a match between the Republic of Ireland and Northern Ireland, when he witnessed horrible scenes of sectarianism. The show was a brilliant piece of writing. Marie Jones loved us, supporting and encouraging us greatly in those early days, and is still a great friend. When we got together all we did was laugh and tell stories about things we'd experienced. It made the hair on Marie's head stand. 'If you don't write those stories into plays I swear I'm stealing them', she said. After that first run of the play, we went on a residential to discuss the future. The result of those discussions was JustUs Theatre Company, a Féile project.

We agreed to produce a play for Féile the following year. That was *Binlids*, a joint production between JustUs and Dubbeljoint, with Pam directing. A team went to work, exploring the options for moving forward. We'd create a training programme, and everyone taking part would get an accredited qualification; a legacy of the company. We got funding for the training, and each person in a role would shadow a professional and begin learning the craft. *Binlids* was to be a semi-professional show, with 'real' actors and production crew; we were nervous and excited.

I talked to Pam; I didn't want to act. I didn't like the attention on stage. She was delighted — she wanted me to write, and shadow her as my professional guide. I was surprised, and truth be told I was touched, but I really was doubtful of her faith. I'd never done anything like this before. I was scared.

As a group, under Pam's direction, we held development sessions and came up with the show's outline. Then I'd go away and research the actual events that were the basis for the scenes. I interviewed dozens of people to get a feel for certain incidents, like the case of the Hooded Men and the Ballymurphy Massacre. I couldn't write anything unless I could feel it; I couldn't feel it if I didn't understand it. I read books and articles. I went to libraries and browsed micro films; this was in the days before the www was widely available, and scanners had only been invented. I was researching and writing for months.

When I was doing all that work I'd no idea it was an actual process that 'real' writers go through — I just needed to understand things so I could write scenes that would make sense to the audience. Eventually we went into rehearsal and at the end of each day I'd go home and do rewrites. It was exhausting, but I loved it — we all did. I remember Bridie, a shining star of our company, telling me one Monday morning she'd been really worried about doing justice to the Máire Drumm scene that Brenda Murphy wrote. She asked what I'd been writing that weekend. I told her the Hooded Men scenes. She said 'ach Margaret, see when I was worried about making an eejit out of Máire Drumm, poor Chrissie was up all night knocking the f#@£ out of Liam Shannon'. We laughed our legs off.

Pam taught me improvisation methods. I loved that, just because you could see the scene taking shape instantly. Pam got me to help our women to develop their characters. She said I'd an eye for detail and could help them 'feel' the part; her faith in me really built my confidence. It was so impressive for me to witness women who'd once been as uncomfortable on stage as I'd been getting more and more confident by the day — and so was I. I wrote and devised most of the script for *Binlids*. Then there was a small number of other writers who added brilliant scenes from their unique experiences — stuff I knew of but not about; their contributions were invaluable.

I don't think we realised how important that work was. We had experienced everything that was written in *Binlids*. It was our life stories. The audiences who came loved the work because it was their lives too. We were a group of women known the length and breadth of the city, and beyond, not usually for our theatre skills. People knew us as ordinary — their family, neighbours, colleagues, their kids' dinner ladies, shop assistants, care workers, advice workers, mammies at the school gates, teachers, students, community workers and various other roles. We were the community telling the community's story in the community's own words. We wanted to do them proud and the stories justice.

After *Binlids*, all our work was semi-professional — but you couldn't tell the difference between our 'amateurs' and the pros; such was the confidence and skills we'd developed. We produced *Forced Upon Us* and *Ordinary People, Extraordinary Lives*. We even ventured into comedy, with *Murphy's Law*, under the brilliant direction of Dan Gordon. Alison, who played the lead, also joined our company. Marie Jones came back to support us too and brought her husband Ian McElhinney to do a workshop with us. That Christmas, a few of us staged a Nativity play in the Felons, and we did some street theatre as well for the Lower Ormeau Residents' Action Group.

Community theatre has many benefits, and as individuals we gained them by the boatload. It builds self-confidence, stimulates imagination, creates empathy, and encourages cooperation and communication skills; it aids concentration and also stimulates fun. Additionally, it's an emotional outlet; it enables the hurt and oppressed to express themselves without censorship. It's a powerful tool for conflict resolution; and it grows an appreciation for arts and culture.

JustUs gave leadership to other groups — 'if we can do it so can you', we'd proclaim. So the company went on to raise its own issues using drama. Many groups and individuals have called on us over the years to support their development, thus enhancing capacity-building within the community. We knew there were more stories to be told — there still are.

Many times I've looked back at my time with Féile and recognised it as one of the most educational times of my life, not in terms of academia — which came later for me — but in terms of myself. I learned more about me in that time than at any other period of my life. As far as I was concerned, I was just doing a job and having a laugh with my friends. I didn't realise the impact it would eventually have. I had a realisation one day of what I'd personally accomplished and thought to myself, 'If I wrote like that and never knew I could, what else might I be able to do that I don't know yet?' So I've tried all sorts.

I think the most special gift I got from Féile has been the people I met and friends I've made along the way. I mentioned very few names in this piece, only naming those I felt I should; I was scared of doing a list and leaving anyone out and hurting their feelings. I also think people should be writing their own stories, so everyone's voices are heard and experiences are captured. I'd love to have written and acknowledged everyone who deserves my appreciation for the contribution I know they made to Féile and in turn West Belfast, but there just wasn't space. Maybe someday I'll find another way to show it.

But there are five people I want to mention. Some were already my friends before Féile, but some weren't. They can't tell their own stories because they aren't with us anymore, but they played significant, unforgettable roles in mine: Siobhán O'Hanlon, Bridie McMahon, 'Uncle' Fra Fox, Pam Brighton and Marc O'Shea. Each and every one of you has made an enormous impression on me that I will never, ever forget — from your love and generosity, your wonderful sense of humour, your skills, expertise and enormous talents in a wide range of areas. Thank you all for being my friends, for all you've taught me, and for the indelible marks you have left on my heart. Unforgettable.

The D&D group

BILL ROLSTON

I joined the Discussions and Debates (D&D) group sometime in the mid-1990s, but it was not my first involvement with Féile and talks. During the very first Féile in 1988 I gave a lecture in Conway Mill on social and political conditions in Belfast in the 1930s. This was based on a book I had just co-written with Ronnie Munck on the topic. It was a daunting prospect; the audience consisted of pensioners who, for the most part, had lived through the events I was talking about — the Outdoor Relief struggle of 1932 and the sectarian riots of 1935. They surely knew more about this than I ever would and would pick up on every mistake I made. It wasn't like that at all. My partial story managed to trigger memories that came pouring out as each of them added whole layers of nuance to what I had to say. It was one of those lovely occasions at Féile where the 'teacher' ends up learning more than the 'students'.

In that first year, I was also involved in Féile's first and only (to date) mural competition. As part of the initial need to show that West Belfast was more than riots and destruction, Bobby Ballagh was called on to go around the murals and judge which was the best. As someone who was presumed to know something about murals, I was privileged to travel with Bobby and Gerry Adams in Adams's armoured taxi as it scraped over ramps and groaned around corners. We went to the murals by Mo Chara in Springhill. Mo Chara's admiration of Jim Fitz-patrick's meticulous paintings of Celtic mythology was clear; Belfast had never seen murals like this. But the prize went to another Mo Chara mural, where he collaborated with some young painters: the portrait of Nelson Mandela, painted that year to celebrate Mandela's 70th birthday.

The pattern was already set in that first year. Féile was not to be simply about music and drama and the sorts of things that festivals normally involved. Discussion and debate were to be at the centre of things, and that was finally formalised in the formation of the D&D group a few years before I was invited to join it. In the decades since, I can recall key speakers, all of whom greatly impressed me in one way or another: Noam Chomsky, Michael Moore, Mary McAleese, Seamus Heaney, Leila Khaled, Doreen Lawrence, Jeremy Corbyn, George Galloway, Mustafa Barghouti, Gareth Pierce, Gary Younge, Michael Mansfield. But this wasn't simply an exercise in celebrity-spotting. Each of these people had important things to say about the wider world and often Féile was the only venue in which people in the North were able to hear them say those things in person. As time went on, there have been more outlets for such speakers. Other festivals and summer schools, as well as annual lectures of NGOs, have brought these speakers to the city. But Féile was innovative in two ways; first, it was doing this when other festivals were not; and second, it was bringing the speakers into West Belfast at a time when government, media, academia and respectable society in general were all working off a mental map which in effect had written in huge letters over West Belfast: 'Here be dragons'.

Syriza in Greece, Podemos in Spain, developments in Palestine or the Basque Country, the American Indian Movement, Black Lives Matter – often the first, or only, time that Belfast has heard directly from such international activists has been at Féile. But the focus was not simply international; there were local needs to be pursued as well. Thus, D&D sought to be inclusive from the very beginning. Attempts were made to invite unionists to show them that the people of West Belfast were not horned and cloven-hooved, and hopefully to have that insight work the other way too. West Belfast Talks Back was a key venue for this. At first it proved almost impossible to entice unionist politicians, and we had to settle for proxies, as it were, in particular Protestant clergy such as John Dunlop and Ken Newell. But in time persistence paid off. Dermot Nesbitt, Reg Empey and other Ulster Unionist party politicians agreed to sit on the panel alongside Sinn Féin during the first Assembly, and during the second, many key Democratic Unionist Party MLAs put in an appearance, with the exception of Rev. Ian Paisley, Peter Robinson, Nigel Dodds and Sammy Wilson. In the early days we used to give a pep talk to the audience before the panellists entered, telling them that the only rule of the evening was respect. Audiences adhered to this rule from the earliest days, even if some of the panellists did not. But even then, they were rarely savaged by the audience. I remember asking Ian Paisley Junior if he thought the audience had given him a hard time; he replied that he had expected much worse.

In time, other people accepted invitations to come into nationalist West Belfast for encounters which would have been unimaginable a few years previously. St Mary's has witnessed some of the most significant encounters: former UVF prisoners talking about their prison experience, PSNI Chief Constable George Hamilton discussing dealing with the past with Martin McGuinness. But not just St Mary's: in an event at Falls Library on the 1994 ceasefires, former loyalist activists and republican activists not only discussed the event but went outside afterwards for a joint photograph in front of the Bobby Sands mural.

But D&D has not just been about bringing the outside in; it has also provided an important platform for insiders to voice issues. Relatives for Justice have staged impressive and emotional discussions on state killings and the pursuit of justice. The Pat Finucane Centre have regularly unveiled the results of their trips to the Public Records Office in London mining long lost documents on collusion. The Ballymurphy Massacre relatives have an annual presence at Féile. These events serve not simply to galvanize the groups concerned but to draw others into the issue, not least others from the outside. I recall George Hamilton being given a private tour in St Mary's of Relatives for Justice's remembrance quilts and meeting some of the relatives who had produced the panels on their dead loved ones. Hamilton was clearly moved by the stories he heard.

To sum it up, I would say that the key thrust of Féile's D&D events has been to introduce West Belfast to the world and the world to West Belfast. The importance of that dual role cannot be underestimated. It is said you do not know a subject if that is the only subject you know. There is indeed a truth to that. Conflict can often lead to isolationism, a feeling of unasked-for uniqueness, even a comfortable sense of victimhood. But this itself is often a reaction to the prejudice that the local is unimportant — that the troubles of West Belfast pale into insignificance compared to those of the Middle East or Darfur (true) and that they are therefore unimportant (untrue). The value of bringing both together is in resonance — even though I know little about X, because I know West Belfast I can identify with X — and there is evidence that that sharing works in both directions. Victims, state killings, collusion, discrimination, apartheid, resistance — these are phenomena that are not unique to West Belfast or Cape Town or Bogotá or Gaza City. So when people from each of these places who have never met before share stories, it is like they are meeting again with distant friends.

Let me give a few stories of some of what I regard as the most memorable occasions when these resonances were in the air.

In 1993, before I joined the D&D group, Noam Chomsky was invited to give a formal lecture on linguistics at the University of Ulster. Although I was employed there, I was neither a professor nor a linguist, so wasn't invited. I had never met Chomsky, but decided to do something incredibly cheeky; I wrote to him and said that he couldn't come to Belfast and miss out on the opportunity to meet and talk to the people of West Belfast. Unbeknown to me, he got a similar letter from Caitríona Ruane, who had worked with his daughter in El Salvador. It looked like a well-planned pincer strategy from which there was no escape. So, Chomsky wrote back to Caitríona and myself saying that if we organized it, he would turn up. He gave an electrifying and wide-ranging lecture to 800 people in the assembly hall in Whiterock College, with 400 others watching through a video link upstairs. A friendship was formed, with an invitation to Chomsky to come back to West Belfast whenever he wanted. So, when he was booked to give a lecture for Amnesty International in Belfast in 2009, he wrote in advance to tell us. We were able to organize another packed meeting in St. Mary's.

There were other occasions when opportunism was the key to getting an international speaker. We got word on one occasion that the film-maker Michael Moore was visiting Ireland. His daughter had just graduated and when asked what she wanted for a present, chose a trip to Ireland. So we contacted Michael and asked him to break his holiday for a day or two to travel up from the south to give a lecture. Amazingly, he agreed! We presumed that there would be a riot if, as usual for our events, this one was unticketed. The event was free, but tickets were handed out in advance from the Féile office on the Falls Road. Over 1000 tickets went in a few hours.

Sometimes the encounters were more accidental but none the less remarkable for that. We showed a documentary film called *The Judge and the General*. It is about Chile after the 1973 coup and focuses on the story of a young left-wing couple from the guerrilla group MIR who were disappeared by the Junta. Years later, activists in Chile persuaded a judge to investigate Pinochet over the couple's disappearance. The judge had been appointed by Pinochet, so the relatives did not hold out much hope. However, he was so shocked by what he found as he started his investigation that he became a convert to human rights and ended up prosecuting Pinochet. It's a moving documentary, but what happened afterwards was even more moving. One of the people in the audience stood up and told us he was from Chile, an exile who had been living in London since the coup. He didn't know about the film or the judge, but had been in the same guerrilla group as the couple; in fact, they had been his commanders. I asked him afterwards had he come from London just to be at the event. But no; he had been on holiday in Belfast for a few days and noticed there was an event about Chile, so he turned up.

Leila Khaled, although invited, did not manage to turn up. She had been a member of the Popular Front for the Liberation of Palestine. In 1970 she was part of a group which hijacked a flight between Rome and Tel Aviv. The plane eventually landed in London where she was taken into custody but later exchanged for hostages taken in a different hijacking. In 2002 she was due to speak at Féile but couldn't get a flight from Amman in Jordan, where she lives, that didn't touch down in Heathrow. So, we had to be content with a video link. She had the audience in stitches when she recounted how she was trying to convince her travel agent in Jordan that she couldn't go through Heathrow. He pointed out to her at one point that she had never any trouble in the past getting a plane to go somewhere different from where it was intended.

Among the most emotional events that I recall, I want to mention three. The first was Gillian Slovo. She is the daughter of anti-Apartheid activists in South Africa, Ruth First and Joe Slovo. Ruth was blown up by a South African parcel bomb in Mozambique, while Joe was head of the military wing of the ANC, Umkhonto we Sizwe (popularly known as the MK). She told the story, also recounted in her book *Every Secret Thing*, of the frustration of herself and her sisters that their parents seemed to be more obsessed with the political cause than with them as family, while at the same time being proud of what their parents had contributed. A daughter of a long-time republican activist sitting beside me turned to me and said, 'How did she know my life story?'

Like many in the audience, I was incredibly conflicted by the lecture given by Izzeldin Abuelaish. His three daughters and a niece were killed by a shell fired by an Israeli tank into their home in Gaza. Yet, he wrote a book titled *I Shall Not Hate*. In his talk it was clear that the title was not mere rhetoric; his commitment to reconciliation was unnerving and challenging for many who listened.

Finally, Sunny Jacobs lived up to her first name with her incredible story of surviving death row in the United States. In later life she met Peter Pringle, one of the last people in Ireland to survive a death sentence, and they became partners. Pensioners now, both of them told their stories with dignity and even humour. Clearly not only did they each have the resilience to survive terrible things, but that resilience seemed multiplied by their relationship.

I started talking about pensioners and in the last paragraph have come back to that. It reminds me that I am now a pensioner myself. I can look back on almost two decades with the D&D group and draw some sort of conclusions. Féile was formed in the dark days of 1988 when the marginalisation and denigration of West Belfast was at its height. We have come a long way, and Féile has been no small part of that. As for the D&D contribution, I would argue that it has been one of the factors that helped the process of conflict transformation here. There is more of a distance to go, so there is more work for the D&D group to do. I have no doubt that the successes of the past will be mirrored in the successes of the future. But then, I would say that, wouldn't I?

Féile: a way of life

CAROL JACKSON

I had just returned to work after the last of my children settled into school. I was working in a café part-time and was advised there was a part-time administrative job with Féile an Phobail. Because I was already involved as a volunteer working in the local festival committee, I decided to check it out. Walking into An Chultúrlann that day for the interview was nerve-racking, but little did I know that this was going to be the start of an absolutely amazing journey that continues to this day.

The place was a hive of activity: Maura Brown, Geordie Murtagh, Chrissie Mhic Siacais and I were all crammed into one room at the top of the old church, which was being used as a hub of organisations for the promotion of the Irish language, including Meánscoil Feirste, the first Irish-medium secondary school in the Six Counties.

I have met many brilliant people — local, national and international — along my journey. I have worked in every part of the organisation, starting with administration and finishing as the Director. I'm still there as a volunteer, working on the discussion and debates programme. Féile an Phobail is one of the most dynamic showcases of our people doing it for themselves. The August Féile began as a response to being demonised by the media after the murders of three IRA volunteers by the SAS in Gibraltar and the murders in Milltown Cemetery. The Féile showcased the positive side of West Belfast and lifted people up during really dark days of conflict.

Féile has been the first for many new cultural initiatives, including: Draíocht, one of the first children's arts festivals in the Six Counties; Oscailt, a community-development programme that ensured people with a disability were included in every element of Féile, from showcasing artists with a disability to ensuring events were accessible for all; the first cross-community St Patrick's Day Carnival parade in Belfast, involving people from north, south, east and west; Féile an Earraigh; Dubbeljoint Theatre Company; West Belfast Film Festival (now Belfast Film Festival); and Triple FM radio station, which was staffed entirely by volunteers and also started life in An Chultúrlann.

My time with Féile has given me some of best times I have ever experienced in my life. It was a very tough job for us all, but was made pleasurable by the brilliant staff and management teams (both paid and voluntary). Teamwork was the central plank that held us all together and enabled Féile to become so successful (we'll not talk about the disaster that brought us down, down, deeper and down, because we certainly got up again). I've met artists who delivered in every art form in both English and Irish, comedians, singers, songwriters, poets and forward-thinking people from every walk of life.

It was a very hard decision for me to leave Féile an Phobail, as it was never a job but a way of life for me and my family, but I knew after ten years that it was time to move over and give someone else a chance to bring new ideas to the festival and continue bringing out the best in the West for locals and visitors alike to enjoy.

My days in Féile radio

VERONICA BROWN

Working on Féile FM/Triple FM gave me the best days of my life. When I think back to then, I always have to smile. The radio was my life and my kids feel it played a big part in their childhood too — they loved it as much as I did. My first memories were of Springvale, at the first ever broadcast. There were live music sessions and I remember food being donated to the station daily in return for advertising. Every day brought something new and the laughter was never-ending. Of course we had a few teething problems, but these were mostly due to the fact the signal was poor in certain areas. We also spent a lot of time moving the aerial around the roof to get the best spot. The ideal signal was when the prisoners in the Lazy K picked us up!

With each broadcast we became more professional and updated our equip-ment. The quality of our advertisements improved greatly and this aided us in generating sponsorship for individual programmes. All money made contrib-uted to the running of the station and paid for the licences. We never received funding, so we relied heavily on this money. I remember we didn't even have paper for writing requests, so we called on the local community groups to donate scrap paper that could be used for this purpose.

Over the 28 days of broadcasting, we had over 200 volunteers involved. This included presenters, technicians and the news team. I remember the youth team getting sponsorship for their programme and I thought I would tell them about it to give them confidence in themselves. The following week, the group asked to speak to me. They proposed using the money to buy CDs, go out for dinner and maybe donate a few pounds to the radio. Imagine their disappointment when I told them it didn't work that way — although I did appreciate the planning and the thought they put into this.

Anne Cadwallader did an amazing job training up our news team and they took their role very seriously. They got the money to purchase a portable mini-disc player and they took to the streets to record vox pops. They also interviewed politicians and other public figures and added clips from the interviews to the news stories. One year we got some funding for marketing materials, and this included cups, t-shirts and stickers. Our young people made a mic cover with our radio stickers. I remember Gerry Adams attending an event and all the media were there and they were asking questions. Gerry was always very supportive of our young people and when he saw the mic, gave our young people priority over the other media providers. This really boosted their confidence.

Fra Coogan was another highlight of my day. He was great craic, although there was occasion when his language wasn't suitable for radio. Cricky was Fra's technician and on more than one occasion Fra was heard live on air telling Cricky he would throw him out the window. Although we knew this was a mess about, I had concerns the listeners wouldn't.

I was so proud of the young people involved in the radio and even today I love to hear how they are getting on. These include our own talented actor, Conor O'Neill, Aislinn Hagan/Higgins, who has her own media company, Dream Media Ireland, and local personality Barra Best, to name but a few. When I meet them and they tell me how they are getting on they all say that their radio experience assisted them to get to where they are today and that they are thankful for the experience gained.

From the foothills of the Black Mountain

Stephen McGlade

We paraded along the Falls Road, beaming with pride, to wild applause from the scores of by-standers out to enjoy the day's fun and craic. It was the first Sunday of August in 1990. I was a 12-year-old from the foothills of the Black Mountain. Family, friends and neighbours cheered as we passed. It was, of course, the opening carnival parade to signal the kick-off of Féile an Phobail – the People's Festival. My friends and I were dressed to impress — and hopefully to win — the best float competition, as we performed on the back of a coal lorry to music from the musical *Grease*. This is my earliest recollection of the West Belfast Festival 30 years ago.

I became involved with Féile, like a lot of kids of our time, through the local youth club and Féile committee. These were established by local people in each district of West Belfast to organise a week-long programme of activities and entertainment during the Féile week. I grew up in the Upper Springfield area, where we were blessed with a wealth of great community leaders and organisers who year-on-year rolled up the sleeves to produce a week of fun, games and light-hearted distraction from the pressures of everyday life in a community living through the Troubles. I, like most, took to it like a duck to water.

We had mountain walks led by our neighbour Terry Enright Snr. With the Troubles, I don't think people had time to see or appreciate the mighty backdrop to where we were living — the Black Mountain. But Terry did. He set out to save the mountain from destruction from quarrying and by capturing people's interest with his sharp intellect, humour and campaigning. His annual Black Mountain walks became a much anticipated pilgrimage for many people over the decades, until his passing in 2012.

Our local community centre, Newhill, was where it all happened. The workers and volunteers there would run a summer scheme for two weeks, followed by a week of festival activities. The place never stopped. By day it was about the kids. By night it was about our parents. Typical socials included a 'Night at the Races', karaoke or even 'Jimmy and his Yamaha'! If the socials weren't at Newhill, they were in the old Newbarnsley Club out back, or up at the Gort na Móna club. Owen McMahon from the well-known folk group, Barnbrack, lived locally too, and was a familiar and great entertainer who would sing many a song and keep the spirits high. Other events included drama, talks and sports.

On another occasion, our neighbour John Neeson, along with well-known republican and Gaeilgeoir Eddie Keenan — both 'characters' — got a group of locals together to learn Irish, and then put on a concert in Gaelic. It turned out to be an all-singing, all-dancing, storytelling affair and the best of craic, enjoyed by everyone who was there.

At this time too, people relied mainly on the *Andersonstown News* for coverage of local events not necessarily of national interest. But some great West Belfast innovators, clearly well ahead of their time, decided we should have a 24/7 news and entertainment service, so they started to broadcast by pirate radio over the week of the festival each year. This is before the internet or Sky TV and also during the period of broadcast censorship banning Sinn Féin from the airwaves, so this way you got to hear the politics and real news! All day long, you could hear authentic music, such as the Wolfe Tones, which no commercial station played. The Long Kesh prisoners, of which there were many, got requests played too, as they listened in from Lisburn.

The local district Féile had been fun year after year, but by now I was at school in the Christian Brothers. There you heard stories about the 'festival at Springhill'. This is where Christy Moore, Brush Shiels, Frances Black, the Century Steel Band and many more all played. On waste ground in the Springhill estate. Well into our teens, my mates and I were determined to get to 'Springhill'. And we did. It was a great week. It closed the year after, as a new housing development was to be built.

The central Féile organisers decided to professionalise and spread their wings by setting up a bigger and better marquee. They started the Debates and Discussions programme and the infamous West Belfast Talks Back event at St Louise's. The exhibitions at St Mary's. The International Food Fayre.

The pirate radio station got their license, becoming Triple FM, and then Féile FM. We were given our own radio show to play out the Manic Street Preachers, REM, The Verve and more, to a whole new audience of West Belfast youth. Fra Coogan became the big hit, though, with his 'golden-oldie' cassette tapes. One of the young people taking telephone requests once gave Fra a song request while on air. It was for Annie who was 'ill'. Fra made a faux pas and played Frank Sinatra for Annie, whom he understood to be 'one hundred and eleven'. There was never a dull moment.

From the foothills of the Black Mountain: *Stephen McGlade*

In late 1999, two of the festival's stalwarts, Siobhán O'Hanlon and Caitríona Ruane, asked me to come and work full-time on the Féile staff for six months. I was 18 and stayed for three years, and I relished every minute of it. I felt I had graduated from our small-time district Féile to the bigtime entertainment league. I was now responsible for organising that opening carnival parade that I started this piece with, alongside a whole series of other events for the main programme. I remember the organising committee were struggling year after year to raise the huge funds needed to stage yet another spectacular festival, and asking myself will Féile be everlasting? I wasn't entirely convinced.

But, 30 years on, it gives us great pride that Féile remains the biggest community festival in Ireland, showcasing the best of talent. It continues to encourage and enthuse all those who remain part of it. Long may it continue.

A staple for our activism and our hope

MARK THOMPSON

August 1998 provided a moment for families affected by state violence and collusion to come together and say 'us too' — we have an experience of conflict that has been ignored: a legacy of impunity. The platform — Féile An Phobail; the venue — St. Mary's College, Falls Road; the event — Forgotten Victims; the context — victimhood, the 'deserving and undeserving'.

The backdrop had been the UK-government-commissioned Bloomfield Report examining the needs of the bereaved and injured of the conflict. Bloomfield focused almost exclusively on the victims of republicans and loyalists, in that order, with a cursory mention that some families made allegations about the role of the state in the deaths of their loved ones. That report also ignored the realities of the need for truth-recovery and accountability, as did our peace accord. This has contributed towards a meta-conflict against the accord and to the maintenance of a false narrative of the past.

Forgotten Victims was the first major Relatives for Justice (RFJ) event in Féile post the peace process. We brought our learning of international conflict processes from South Africa to Latin America that grappled with and found solutions to similar post-conflict issues. Importantly, the event heard voices that had been silent for decades. Neilly Rooney, whose nine-year-old son Patrick was the first child to be killed in the conflict, broke his long silence by describing publicly that awful evening, as did several relatives of people killed during the days of internment, individually speaking and then for the first time meeting afterwards in what would eventually become, with RFJ support, not least from Andrée Murphy, the Ballymurphy Massacre Group. I remember Liam Quinn standing holding a picture of his brother Frank as he spoke, the emotion still raw. The scene was captured the next day on the front page of the *Irish News*.

It was also when RFJ coined the phrase 'No hierarchy of victimhood' and when those families stood up and said 'us too … we have an experience of loss also'. The following year, 1999, RFJ held a public hearing, on the July 1972

Springhill Massacre carried out by the British Army, which for the first time brought all the families, survivors and witnesses together to chronologically record and document these five killings, which included the killings of three children and a parish priest. Féile has always provided an important platform in which marginalised voices are heard and valued, where new creative, imaginative and challenging ideas are encouraged, discussed and debated. Where activism happens. Where we try to be solution-focused. And this type of activism and these qualities are central to RFJ, so Féile was and remains a staple for our activism and our hope.

Outside of RFJ, I had the privilege of organizing several events in 1997. This included putting together a daily, hour-long current-affairs-type radio programme, in which those interviewed also chose music and discussed their lives more generally. I had Martin Meehan interview Joe and Annie Cahill about their lives, imprisonment, escapes, life on the run, how they met and fell in love and survived it all — it was a personal highlight. Joe Austin interviewed Susan Duffy about the incarceration of her husband Collie and several murder bids, including at their home, their campaign for justice and the impact it had on their young family. Joe also tackled the issue of parading and interviewed Derry Apprentice Boys spokesperson Tommy Chivers along with nationalist residents, thus getting beneath the surface of the issue. Several RFJ figures, including Clara Reilly and the late Eilish McCabe from Tyrone, spoke about their experiences of conflict and campaigns for justice. This also got beyond the headlines. And on the Friday, Fergus O'Hare interviewed Gerry Adams, which is always fascinating for people of all persuasions. And we played his favourite songs, with classics from Luke Kelly to Leonard Cohen.

Mart Holland, Hodgies, Tony Carlisle and the crew at the radio station were marvellous and we all sat hanging on every word during the Annie and Joe Cahill interview. Even the late Fra Coogan, who also hosted a daily show, remarked on that particular interview. I've a picture of us all, post the interview, marking that day.

Another major event was the launch of our Remembering Quilt, a derivative of the International Aids Quilt and the great US tradition of quilting, post the American Civil War, where mothers, widows and daughters came together, not just to quilt but also to heal, bond and learn to live again after loss. A form of counselling and therapy before the terms existed. Our quilt was similarly based and involved hundreds of families, thousands of relatives, and was inclusive and led the way in terms of equality of loss and memory. Gerry Adams spoke at the launch, also in St. Mary's. However, there was much speculation about decommissioning and thus the world's press were present too as they chased any sense of an announcement. And so families who made squares in the Remembering

Quilt stood beside the assembled world media and its launch featured briefly in world news, including in Spanish, French, German, Russian, and other languages, as international correspondents spoke to families in the absence of an announcement.

RFJ had been founded in April 1991 in Dungannon and several of its founding members were also the driving force within the Association for Legal Justice (ALJ) and the United Campaign Against Plastic Bullets (UCAPB). UCAPB was in direct response to the murder of John Downes outside Connolly House on 12 August 1984, when the RUC attacked unarmed civilians as they peacefully gathered to mark the anniversary of internment; the events from which Féile would eventually emerge. And so, from 1985 onwards, UCAPB organized and held vigils outside of Andersonstown RUC barracks on John's anniversary and in memory of all those killed and maimed by rubber and plastic bullets. This vigil, with the formidable Clara Reilly and bereaved families, is a steadfast of Féile. We always remember too the late Emma Groves, blinded by a rubber bullet, who campaigned tirelessly against plastic bullets and who we described as West Belfast's First Lady. Emma travelled the world with Clara and campaigning families. We've always said that the former Andersonstown RUC Barracks site, now a green, with the barracks thankfully gone, should be named after and dedicated to Emma and the families.

RFJ has organised and participated in numerous Féile events directly connected to our work, on themes of truth, justice, accountability, healing, and recovery, involving local, national and international voices. We had internationally recognised investigative journalist John Ware — who has made many ground-breaking programmes on the conflict, not least regarding collusion — interview former PSNI chief Hugh Orde about dealing with the past. Clara Reilly, during her excellent introduction and scene-setting of the event, told him straight that he wouldn't be referred to as 'Sir Hugh' whilst in the West, which drew laughter. Orde's often-cavalier approach included having senior PSNI personnel in attendance and sitting on tenterhooks while waiting for 'hand-grenade' questions to be thrown their way.

And we've always had smaller yet equally important events and exhibitions, where families we support share personal memories of their loved ones killed and express their journeys of healing and recovery through the medium of art, pottery, crafts and photography. The standard of talent on display is something to behold and never ceases to amaze and inspire.

Building international solidarity and strengthening international relations around human rights are key to advancing national causes. Undoubtedly, the Féile platform and resource has enhanced and strengthened this dimension of our work, forging links with Palestine, the Sikhs, South Africa, Latin America and beyond. Féile is now a significant international event, attracting global attention and participation. Consequently we too access that arena in terms of the ability to attract key figures and wider audiences and that can only be good for our membership and the issues they continue to face. Féile too must also be about celebration and we must allow for carnival in our revolution whilst we discuss and debate crucially important issues that are at the heart of everyday life. We should find a balance: to live and enjoy, yet not forget. The diversity of Féile in that respect can be a metaphor for how we should try to live our lives.

Féile abú!

Scribes

DANNY MORRISON

While many local writers' groups had put on readings of poetry and prose in pubs and clubs in the early days of Féile, we never had a dedicated event aimed at inviting in established authors to read from their work.

Carol Jackson had just taken over as Féile director from Caitríona Ruane. For the previous two years, I had been teaching creative writing in classes at Conway Mill and I mentioned to the new director that I thought it would be great if we could lure into West Belfast some major writers to do readings, but in an intimate setting, without airs and graces. Carol's reaction was — Go For It!

So, on Thursday, 9 August, 2001, we had our first Scribes at the Rock. Among the authors were Eoin McNamee and Pat McCabe, who not only read from his Booker-shortlisted novel, *The Butcher Boy,* but did an astonishing re-enactment of scenes from the book to the packed and gobsmacked upstairs lounge of the Rock Bar. Also on the bill was one of the most creative musicians in Ireland, Duke Special, who returned a few years later for another Scribes, to talk about the art of song writing: where do lyrics come from and which comes first — the words or the music?

Scribes has become a niche event in Féile, always on a Thursday afternoon, always in the Rock Bar, with a loyal audience of around one hundred and fifty people. The list of those who have taken part is huge and includes writers, poets, screenplay writers, theatre directors and actors, all of whom have testified to the wonderful atmosphere and the warm welcomes they receive. These have included: Tim O'Grady, Roddy Doyle, Holly McNish, Irvine Welsh, Evelyn Conlon, Alexei Sayle, Medbh McGuckian, Linton Kwesi Johnson, Peter Sheridan, Geraldine Hughes, Paul Laverty, Pauline McLynn, Hugo Hamilton, Gillian Slovo, Conal Creedon, Brian Kennedy, Marian Keyes, Tony Macaulay, Philomena Lynott, Kevin Barry, Ronan Bennett, Dominic Dromgoole, Levi Tafaris, Paul Howard, Michael Patrick MacDonald, Marina Lewycka, Michael Harding, Kevin Higgins and Shane Connaughton.

Two hilarious contributors were the poets, the surrealistic Dan Eggs, and Les Barker, the title of whose poems speak for themselves: 'Cosmo the Fairly Accurate Knife Thrower'; 'Guide Cats for the Blind'; and 'Dachshunds with Erections'. But the most hilarious, yet poignant of Les Barker's poems is about the sinking of the Titanic, told from the perspective of a sad and lonely polar bear whose family was *on* the iceberg and who goes to the White Star Line's HQ in Liverpool and asks:

Have you got any news of the iceberg? My family were on it you see. Have you got any news of the iceberg? They mean the whole world to me. My wife and my children were coming from Greenland, to be by my side in the zoo. Belinda's my wife, and the eldest's called Bernard. And Billy, well, he's only two.

On another occasion, guest speaker Pete Hamill, the American journalist and novelist, and I arrived early, so I took him into the public bar downstairs even though he no longer drinks and alcohol was a subject of his award-winning memoir, *A Drinking Life*. As we stood at the bar with our soft drinks, Pete experienced a wave of déjà vu and suddenly remembered that he'd been here before. He said that in November 1963 he came back to Ireland with his Belfast-born father, who wanted to visit the city one more time before he died. They had been on a pub crawl and ended up in the Rock Bar. And there, up in the corner, he said, pointing to the huge flat screen TV, was a black and white TV, and on that TV came a newsflash announcing that President Kennedy had been assassinated in Dallas, Texas. The hairs stood up on the back of my neck as he re-lived that moment all those years before.

Local writers who have spoken at Scribes include Pat McDermott and Patricia Gormley, both from my creative writing class, and Tim Brannigan, whose brilliant memoir, *Where Are You Really From?*, about being black and growing up on the Falls Road, has been optioned by Oscar-winning producer John Lesher (director of *Birdman* and *Fury*).

In class Pat McDermott was quiet but his work was often funny, subversive or enigmatic. At Scribes, he read this lovely thoughtful piece about 'the first time' and it is still one of my favourites.

My Dear Charlene
And did he break the spell my dear Charlene
While in the grass and flower blooms you lay
And did he take away that fragile dream
And turn the world a deeper shade of grey

And did you think of all the world you knew
Which vanished in the second now just past
And did you see the sky no longer blue
But made blue, by some natural cause or cast

And did you think on walking back again
No longer hand in hand but side by side
That what you lost was more than what you gained
And could you understand why they had lied.

You listened to the story like the rest
But now you see 'twas only spoke in jest.

Back in 2001, Patricia Gormley also publicly read for the first time; it was one of her hilarious short-stories about a teenage daughter and her friends. Since then, Patricia has written and performed in many of her own plays, including *The Bus Run* and *I'll Tell Me Ma* (the story of four generations of a West Belfast family and the ups and downs they face), which have played at Belfast's Mac and the Lyric Theatre, amongst other prestigious venues.

I'm proud of Scribes and the fact that, although a small event, it attracts the most prestigious of writers on the Irish literary scene and beyond. And, that while local people have the opportunity to hear at first hand major writers read from their work, those writers themselves experience a little bit of the hospitality, warmth and friendliness of West Belfast and go away as ambassadors for a once beleaguered, now incredibly proud and confident community.

The News Team

ANNE CADWALLADER

There were not a few butterflies in my tummy when I walked into Blackstaff Mill in the mid 1990s to face a room full of young faces — all wanting to learn about radio journalism. I knew only too well that most young people in West Belfast had a somewhat jaundiced view of journalism — a view formed by frequent media assumptions about them and their community.

But we had a mere six weeks or so to form a volunteer news team for Triple FM (Féile's own community station) that could deliver hourly three-minute bulletins that would be broadcast live across the city from 6am to 10pm. We had no time to argue about the rights and wrongs of mainstream press and broadcasting. It was all hands on deck — and this was for real. Two hours, one evening a week. Rising to many hours every day. We set about the basics of radio news reporting.

We learned about the 'inverted triangle' of news (put the important bits first). We learned about news sources (we called the RUC press office if we heard sirens screaming along the Falls). We learned about being impartial, or as impartial as possible. We knew they would be listening to us on the Shankill and, anyhow, sectarian language was totally unacceptable in principle. We learned to write short sentences. We learned about emphasising the most significant words in those sentences. We learned about breathing in the right places. We learned about how grammar and cadences fit into spoken radio news. We learned that we would hate the sound of our own voices on air (at first) but we'd get used to it. They learned about time. How seconds and minutes can tick by and, suddenly, scared silly, you're in front of that unforgiving microphone again to read the next bulletin.

As the weeks went by, the class of youngsters gradually, gradually, began to realise they could do this. When they read their first news bulletin, lights came on behind their eyes. This was fun, this was real and they could do it!

They were told to think and feel like journalists. To have the confidence of asking questions of the great and the good, like journalists. They were taught to fear no-one and nothing. They were there on behalf of the public, the community, to ask the hard questions, to read the news (and the sport and the weather and the traffic reports) and to demystify the process of news gathering and broadcasting.

It was certainly not all plain-sailing. I tried in vain to tell them that, when it came to reading their own names at the end of each of their reports, they shouldn't tail off into a mutter.

'Speak it loud and speak it proud. Say your own name. You've done the work. You've read the news. Your name matters. This is your payback time. Speak your name LOUDLY at the end of your report'.

It didn't make any difference. They still muttered their own names.

But, in another way, it DID make a difference. The shy young people of a month or so ago developed into far more confident voices. Friendships developed. Even romances. Great fun was had in the short 55 minutes between one bulletin and the next.

Their parents and school friends heard them on the radio, reading the news. They heard each other in taxis and in shops. And they didn't sound too bad at all! Some of them accompanied me one summer as I reported on rioting along the Springfield Road. Rule number one was, watch out for flying rocks and bottles and — above all — keep yourself safe. Injured reporters read no news. It wouldn't be allowed now, of course. Health and safety.

One summer, we roasted in the attic above a chemist's shop in Andytown. Another summer we had to clear out the rats from a dingy basement in the Lower Falls. We ran out of paper and pens and newspapers and printers. But we persevered. I thought the pride that I had felt when I heard the teams reading the news they had written themselves was incomparable. Then a mother told me that her son's attitude to his studying had changed since he'd joined 'The News Team'. He was now working hard and determined to succeed.

And that taught me one of life's most important lessons. Give a young person confidence in their ability, and they will amaze you. Persuade them that they are capable of doing a high-profile, prestigious job — and they will adapt and succeed. Many of those young people went on to work hard and study and compete for well-paid jobs in mainstream media and communications (yes, you know who you are and I'm not going to name you all). I could not be prouder of them and so grateful for what they gave me back.

Féile gave them that opportunity. Without Féile they — and I — would never have been able to learn from each other. Féile changed their lives. And mine.

Féile an Phobail: the personal is political

PHIL SCRATON

'*She ate with her fingers. They'd taunt and laugh at her ... blowing smoke through the door ... She tried to hang herself and three of us saw her getting out of the ambulance. They walked her across the tarmac in February with a suicide blanket on. They all had riot gear on. She was crying. They were bringing her back from hospital and she was put back in the punishment block. We just kept our heads down. Just did our time.*'

I read these words at the opening of my early afternoon Féile Radio programme. It was a moving extract from a harrowing interview with a woman prisoner in the Mourne House Women's Unit, Maghaberry jail. She described the appalling treatment endured by an emotionally disturbed older woman. Held in a punishment cell as 'uncooperative', the older woman was epileptic, diabetic and carried a colostomy bag. Profound inhumanity on our doorstep in the mid-2000s. This was the first part of my scripted broadcast on women in prison, ending with Christy Moore's *On the Bridge*. Leaving Conway Mill a couple of hours later, I met two women and their children waiting for me. They'd dropped over simply to thank me for exposing the inhumane conditions and neglectful treatment at the jail. Each had a sister inside.

Throughout our first years at Féile we lived near Liverpool, staying in Belfast with our close friends Anna Eggert and Bill Rolston. Bill was immersed in arranging talks and debates alongside his own engaging lectures. Other than the exception of the year we were turned back by not-so-EasyJet at Speke Airport, Féile was scheduled into our summers. Its intensity reminded me of teaching Open University Summer School — the seemingly oblivious wider world continuing its daily routine while our lives were determined only by the programme. Each day bringing a roller-coaster of emotions. We wandered the corridors and rooms of St Mary's University College viewing the art and installations alongside the Ballymurphy Families' quest for justice. The tragic beauty of the

Remembering Quilt — the final words of the beautiful poem written by Micheál Gallagher: '*A square of cloth, a love, a life / A memory sewn on patchwork dye / We'll proudly piece those threads of history back into the fabric of our lives*.' Then to political debates, guest speakers, the health sessions, Scribes at the Rock, West Belfast Talks Back, ending up, via *Cultúrlann*, at a comedy night or a gig. We cried, we remembered, we debated, we laughed, we sang, we slept (briefly), 'occasionally' drank … and we returned home, back to work for a rest!

In 1999 the first edition of my book *Hillsborough: The Truth* was published and I gave my first Féile talk, hosted by Andrée Murphy, Clara Reilly and Mark Thompson at Relatives for Justice (RFJ). It was in a room at the RFJ offices, attended by less than 20 people. I seem to remember Flair Campbell and Sara Boyce, now close friends, were there. At that time we had no idea that we would soon move to Belfast. Nor that over a decade later the Hillsborough families' fight for justice would lead to the Hillsborough Independent Panel and then to new inquests. Throughout that period, I gave several Hillsborough talks. I'll never forget a night in St Aidan's — an impressive Ballymurphy turn-out for Hillsborough's 20th Anniversary. The hall was packed — so many Liverpool shirts — men and women sitting alongside children on small school chairs.

Years later, following the Hillsborough Panel's ground-breaking findings, new inquests were under negotiation. Hillsborough families travelled over to share a platform with Ballymurphy families, Pádraig Ó Muirigh and myself. 'Ballymurphy: Adopting the Hillsborough Model?' was an intense, moving and uplifting session. Collectively, the families' unwavering persistence demonstrated a powerful unity of purpose in memory of loved ones lost. To appropriate Antonio Gramsci's memorable phrase, 'optimism of the spirit' filled the room. At that moment no-one anticipated the outcome of the Hillsborough inquests. Following the Panel's report, the original verdicts of accidental death were overturned. The new inquests were in session for two years, the longest in legal history. No doubt exhausted, their lives 'on hold', the jury concluded that all who died had been killed unlawfully. 25 strongly-worded criticisms were directed towards the authorities, 15 against the police. The Ballymurphy families drew hope from this 'victory' and, in 2016, Féile hosted Dan Gordon's remarkable, BAFTA-winning film, *Hillsborough*, at the Omniplex.

In the early 2000s, across West Belfast neighbourhoods, there was profound concern about the 'antisocial behaviour' of children and young people. Not part of Féile, a packed public meeting was held in St Mary's. Not long living in the North, I spoke about draconian policing of young people over the water and how through 'crime and disorder' legislation they were fast-tracked to detention without having committed a criminal offence. The indefatigable Paddy Kelly spoke about the institutional abuse of children's rights. We argued that the full impact of drink, drugs, unemployment, the conflict's legacy and a deep sense of worthlessness among young people had to be understood and addressed. Yes, young people's outward behaviour was antisocial, even threatening. Internalised, however, their sense of failure and hopelessness led to self-harm and the loss of life. Not everyone was sympathetic. Then, from the floor, came an impassioned, informed, no-holds-barred analysis. It was received with profound respect and ringing applause. Those seeking reactionary solutions through formal or informal policing, those who dismissed young people as 'scum', were halted in their tracks. It was the first time I'd witnessed Terry Enright in full flight.

Reflecting fully on my Féile experiences and their impact on our lives personally, socially and politically, is challenging. One thing for sure — they centre on people. When I first met Terry I had no idea about the Hatchet Field, nor Black Mountain and his fight, on behalf of the people who live beneath its summit, to retrieve access from the restrictions imposed by the British State. For many, Terry's walks became a defining element of the Féile experience. In his memory the walk, via the 'slippy slope', is now an annual Boxing Day event — most recently with our grand-daughter, Lotte.

It was during an early visit to Féile that we met Mary Enright, hearing from others about her pivotal role in setting up the Falls Women's Centre. Soon after, we discovered that in 1998 Terry and Mary's son, Terry Óg, had been murdered by Loyalist paramilitaries. His brothers, Liam, Niall and Feargal became good friends. I worked with Niall on the board of Include Youth and have seen at close quarters his unswerving dedication to young people across the communities. It was a great honour to write the foreword to Feargal's brilliant book, *Language, Resistance and Revival*. For those outside the community, Féile offers a catalyst for great friendship.

We first met Laurence McKeown in 1995, at an international conference held in Crossmaglen GAC. The British Army had commandeered the ground adjacent to the clubhouse. Throughout the day, talks were forced to pause as helicopters came and went. It was a remarkable backdrop to Laurence recounting his profoundly personal and political journey — Long Kesh, imprisonment, the hunger strikes and education in the H-Blocks. His knowledge, understanding and scholarship were matched by remarkable humility. That year within Féile, Laurence founded the West Belfast Film Festival. Five years later, it developed into the now internationally recognised Belfast Film Festival, directed by Michele Devlin. Laurence's plays, books and articles are a significant part of a history exemplifying Féile's community-based achievement. His remarkable *H3* stands, ahead of Steve McQueen's *Hunger*, as the definitive film on the hunger strike and the appalling circumstances in which ten men — his friends — died.

In the development of Féile theatre, Pam Brighton's direction, not least with Dubbeljoint, made a significant contribution. Alongside her other plays, Brenda Murphy's *Two Sore Legs* took her to the Edinburgh Fringe and beyond. It was about this time we met Niamh Flanagan, whose contribution to the arts in the North also extends beyond Féile. Rooted in West Belfast, the Féile's wider literary contribution is one of its great achievements. This includes Danny Morrison's writing. Danny has been pivotal in bringing authors to Féile, not least the annual afternoon session Scribes at the Rock, a literary event that has people queuing in the street. It is difficult to select a short-list of fine authors — be it fiction or autobiography. Who would have thought Michael Moore would agree to talk at Féile — as long as there was no admission charge? It became the 'hottest' free ticket in town! Noam Chomsky, Tim Robbins, Seamus Heaney, Gary Younge — the list goes on.

We all have our 'stand-out' moments. The calmness of Sunny Jacobs' PJ McGrory lecture on her outstanding book *Stolen Time* was memorable, as she talked through her devastating experience of death row in the USA for a crime she didn't commit. Her openness, support for other prisoners and campaign against the death penalty remain inspirational. As does the life of Izzeldin Abuelaish. His book *I Shall Not Hate* recounts the deliberate, callous shelling of his house in Gaza by an Israeli tank. He survived, but three of his daughters and niece were killed. Ironically, Izzeldin had been the first Palestinian doctor to work in an Israeli hospital, often forced by Israeli guards to wait 24 hours at check-points as he moved between work and home. Telling such profound life histories demonstrates the 'reach' of Féile beyond community and beyond Ireland. Embracing established projects and new ideas, it engages both locally and internationally with recent history.

In 2004, Geraldine Finucane delivered a PJ McGrory lecture on the long campaign for justice following the 1989 murder of her husband Pat Finucane. In a deeply personal talk, Geraldine exposed the full political context of state collusion in what amounted to an execution in the family home. Soon after, I asked Geraldine to open an international conference at Queen's. From the reception she received and the correspondence that followed, it was evident that her talk had a significant impact on those who attended, not least beyond the island of Ireland. As with Hillsborough, the denial of justice and the refusal to pursue cases — inquests or prosecutions — expose the State's failure to meet its constitutional responsibility. In this vein, Bernadette McAliskey's more recent contribution to the Frank Cahill Memorial Lecture was memorable, her sharp analysis and quick wit, as ever, stimulating informed debate. From public debate, back to film. RFJ screened the Alex Gibney ESPN documentary *Ceasefire Massacre*, which investigated the 1994 UVF attack at O'Toole's Heights Bar in

Loughinisland that left six men dead. Investigative journalist Barry McCafferty and human rights solicitor Niall Murphy, both central to the film, discussed its making and significance. In 2018, a more comprehensive version, *No Stone Unturned*, was premiered at the New York Film Festival.

Films are not the only visual images associated with Féile. The work of Danny Devenny and that of his fellow muralists is legendary. Each year during Féile their scaffolding fronts the International Wall. The 1916 Easter Rising commemorative mural, complete with Liver Bird insignia, was yet another significant contribution to public memorialisation. They also travelled to Liverpool to paint wonderful murals in our city, not least the Liverpool-Ireland tribute on the city's Irish Centre. Bill Rolston's four mural volumes, *Drawing Support*, chronicle political shifts across the North over three decades. Beyond his regular Féile talks, they have brought his scholarship deserved international recognition. Stuart Borthwick's excellent photography led to publication of his murals book, *The Writing on the Wall*, launched at Féile and at Merseyside's Writing on the Wall Festival.

This brief review of my personal experiences, shared with family and friends, illustrates the inescapable intensity of Féile. Days spent moving between events, often while they're in session, seem to merge within a parallel time zone. You even forget to eat. At the end of another engaging discussion, realising that dehydration is slowing my brain (or maybe it is age), I nick a bottle of water from the speakers' table. Or, if there's time, drop by Cultúrlann to grab a bun, a cup of tea and more intense discussion. Night follows day. Many stand-out, often involving fine music. Clonard, where the brilliance of the music goes some way to alleviating the numbness induced by hard pews. My most memorable nights include the Harlem Gospel Choir, Altan, Brian Kennedy, Sharon Shannon, Mary Coughlan, Christy Moore and, of course, at different times, the Blacks — Frances and Mary. It was here that I first heard the great musicians, Brame di Corsica.

Then the leisure centre sessions — Beechmount and Andersonstown (for me, the Falls Park tent has lost the camaraderie and proximity of the long tables and the jugs of Guinness/Murphy's). Who could forget such great performances — Afro Celts, Hothouse Flowers, Eileen Ivers, Luka Bloom, Solas, Proclaimers and the Afro-Cuban All Stars. The latter, complete with entourage, must have cost a fortune. Maybe it's apocryphal, but I heard on reliable information (or not!) that they were instructed to play by Fidel himself. Given the size of the band, that must have been some backstage rider! When The Beat played I ran to the stage like a teenager to show Ranking Roger my 'Stand Down Margaret' badge. 'Wicked, man', was his mid-verse response. Not to forget our fine local musicians and singers, whose reputations are now deservedly international — particularly my good friends Barry Kerr and Gráinne Holland.

One night in Andersonstown Leisure Centre will never leave me. The gig opened with the wonderful Féile Women's Singing Group led by Anna Newell; as ever, stunning and uplifting. Then came the brilliant Karan Casey, whom I first heard in Solas. She arrived with her recently born baby. Typically forthright, she apologised profusely for 'leaking' during the performance! Eddi Reader and her band topped the bill. After the gig, I was due to interview Eddi for Féile Radio. While she recovered from her usual energetic performance, I spotted Karan sitting on the 'Green Room' sofa — breast-feeding. Without a moment's hesitation, she agreed to an interview. Throughout the broadcast, you could hear her baby feeding away. Then I recorded Eddi. I had all her albums and I confessed to being a 'fan'. Like Karan, she was easy to interview and, in the years since, we've become close friends. I often wonder whatever happened to those memorable recordings?

So, full circle to Féile Radio. I forged lasting friendships with those I met at the station, not least Emma Mullen, and also Aislinn Hagan. I have transcripts of all seven broadcasts, repeated year-on-year with updates. Each has eight music tracks and is about eleven thousand words of script. They are: *Hillsborough*; *Women in Prison*; *The 'War on Terror'*; *The Politics of Truth and Official Inquiries*; *Dunblane – A Decade On*; *The Roots of Race and Sectarian Hate*; *The Politics of Children's Rights*. The scripts became the foundation for my book, *Power, Crime and Criminalisation*. Ten lines from Christy Moore's *On the Bridge* introduce the final chapter.

My experience of Féile includes the 'unfinished business', as Bill Rolston names it, which is central to so many families seeking long-overdue inquests and thorough inquiries into the deaths of loved ones. The close relationship between the festival and the pursuit of justice has been a constant theme. Its pursuit, however, extends beyond the community and the conflict. When Linda Moore and I gave a Féile talk on our research revealing the appalling conditions endured by women prisoners, it met with some opposition because of their 'ordinary' rather than 'political' status. Yet the circumstances of incarceration and the conditions under which prisoners and detainees are held are political — administered in 'our' name, funded by 'our' taxes. Refugee, asylum seeker, shop-lifter, lifer, drug-user, mother, daughter, father, son ... in prison a strip search is a strip search is a strip search. All incarceration is a political act.

Féile, then, has been part of our lives before and throughout our time in Belfast. It has given us great pleasure and created significant challenges. It has enriched our lives and brought our work recognition across communities and across the islands. Without Féile, I doubt whether my partner, Deena Haydon, or I would have had the honour of each delivering the annual lecture in memory of Harry Holland. English speakers only, we have been welcomed at events at Coláiste Feirste and Glór na Móna promoting and securing the future of my ancestors' first language. From its roots as a community-based festival, reflecting Terry Enright's commitment, Féile has generated and consolidated inclusivity across communities beyond West Belfast's boundaries.

Providing our people with a life affording scope

Pádraig Ó Muirigh

The ancient Greeks defined happiness as the 'exercise of vital powers along the lines of excellence in a life affording them scope'. Whilst my childhood growing up in West Belfast in the 1980s was certainly a happy one, the fulfilment of that objective was increasingly difficult for many, including my own clann, in the face of widespread economic and social deprivation. Unemployment and poverty were the norm; opportunities for a life affording scope were few and far between.

These injustices sprang from deliberate British Government (and unionist) policies for many decades. Commenting on British Government ideas to tackle poverty and unemployment in West Belfast, in a 1987 memo to British Secretary of State Tom King, Ken Bloomfield, head of the Civil Service, famously described our community as 'alienated from normal civilised behaviour' and having a 'ghetto mentality'. It was also around this time that funding was withdrawn from community and social enterprises across the North and in particular West Belfast. We were a demonised community. These colonial tactics were best summed up by a senior British soldier, in a conversation with a Clonard priest, when he described our community as a 'tube of toothpaste that would be squeezed until it delivered the IRA'.

In March 1988 I experienced my first loss when a relative, Dan McCann, was executed in Gibraltar with Mairead Farrell and Seán Savage. Their long journey home, the attack on the funeral cortege by loyalist Michael Stone, and the deaths that followed in the days and weeks afterwards are tattooed in my memory. It was one of the darkest periods of our recent history.

Out of that darkness, an idea was born — or maybe it was an idea that was rekindled — which led to the first Féile in August 1988. Those Féile founders and visionaries recognised that enabling our community to mark off a corner of the world in which its people could express themselves, put their best foot forward and welcome the world in to see for itself who we were and what we stood for, was our best retort to the British direct-rule ministers and their officials.

My earliest and fondest memories of the Féile are the street parties: local rock bands playing on a stage at a street corner and, at International Night in the old Conway Mill, the Corsican traditional band Cantu Populu Corsu belting out international revolutionary tunes such as 'Companero' and the Italian partisan anthem 'Bella Ciao'. I attended my first concert at Féile — the legend Bap Kennedy and Energy Orchard inside Beechmount Leisure Centre — and on another occasion I watched Shane MacGowan sing outside the same venue, on the playing pitches.

As I grew older, I became more interested in the Féile debates and discussions programme. The annual PJ McGrory Lecture was formative in the development of my career as a lawyer, as I was exposed to human rights advocates and campaigns from all over the world. Over the years, I attended hundreds of talks and lectures at Féile, but a few stand out. The brave Carmen Proetta, who witnessed the Gibraltar assassinations, told a Féile audience about how she was demonised by the right-wing tabloids after she spoke out. The investigative journalist, Gary Younge, mesmerised the crowd with his talk about the origins of the Black Lives Matter movement and racism in the US.

The Féile has always been a platform for victims of the conflict, when a hostile justice system delayed and denied them justice. There is an annual presence by the Ballymurphy families, the McGurk's Bar campaign and NGOs such as Relatives for Justice and the Pat Finucane Centre. These families have also drawn inspiration from the campaigns of other victims of British colonial policy from around the world. John Halford, the lawyer for 24 unarmed Chinese plantation workers slaughtered by Scots Guards at a Malayan rubber plant in Batang Kali in December 1948, gave a powerful presentation on their legal fight in British courts to secure a public inquiry into the circumstances of the massacre.

Dan Leader, the lawyer for elderly Kenyans who were tortured during the Mau Mau revolt against British colonial rule in the 1950s and 1960s, gave a talk on their landmark legal victory in the High Court in London, which led to the British Government paying out £20m to more than 500 victims of torture. Their inspirational story reminded me of the verse by Seamus Heaney, 'History says Don't hope / On this side of the grave, / But then, once in a lifetime / The longed-for tidal wave / Of justice can rise up / and hope and history rhyme.'

My involvement with the Féile has evolved over the years, from attending street parties as an 11-year-old boy, to working on security at Féile events after UDA threats, to my appointment as a director on the Féile Board and member of the Féile Debates & Discussions (D&D) committee. I have had the pleasure of working with Féile stalwarts, such as Bill Rolston, Jim Gibney, Carol Jackson and Claire Hackett.

The D&D group has carried on that Féile tradition of being brave and bold. One of our mottos is that Féile 'does firsts'. In recent years, I have introduced Martin McGuinness and the first PSNI Chief Constable, George Hamilton, to speak at Féile. I also helped organise an event where Orange Order leader Mervyn Gibson shared a platform with my father, Sean Murray, a former IRA prisoner. Perhaps my proudest moment with Féile was introducing Michael Mansfield QC to give the 2016 PJ McGrory Lecture. It was a fitting tribute to PJ, a fearless advocate for the people of West Belfast.

We have also strived to keep up with the rapidly changing political landscape and organised talks on Brexit and its implications for us all. We have been a platform for discussions and debates about how a future United Ireland might look, in the eyes of politicians, unionists, republicans, economists, artists, and sportspeople.

Many of those involved in the birth of Féile have learned to find their own advancement in the search of the advancement of others. Some have stayed with Féile and many others have gone on to give their skills and energy to the community in other roles and responsibilities. Their contribution to this proud community has been invaluable. Whilst Féile hasn't eradicated all West Belfast's social and economic problems — their causes deep and complex — it is not an exaggeration to say that the festival has played an important role in reconciliation and building relationships across our divided community. It has sent forth a tiny ripple that, with other likeminded initiatives, can 'build a current that can sweep down the mightiest walls of oppression … ' If I was asked to define Féile's greatest achievements, I would say that it has provided a voice to our community, our young people, victims of the conflict, and our artists, and it has helped bring some happiness and joy to West Belfast in some difficult times. To misquote the famous Irish playwright, George Bernard Shaw, 'Some people see things and say, "why?" The people of West Belfast dreamed things that never were, and said "Why Not?"'

Here's to another 30 years of Féile an Phobail!

Féile: something for everyone

Aislinn Higgins (Hagan)

Dressed in my little twin-set and pedal-pushers, I kissed my dad goodbye. Armed with my notebook and pen, I ascended the stairs of Blackstaff Mill to attend my first Triple FM news team meeting. It was 1998 and unknown to my 13-year-old self, that short climb was the first step to what would soon shape the rest of my life.

It all began a week earlier, when Martin Óg Flynn started his annual fund-raising campaign across West Belfast, visiting local businesses, trying to drum up money to keep Triple FM on the air as it approached its summer schedule. First up on his list was my dad's travel agency, Tower Travel, which was based on the Falls Road. 'Gerry, any chance of sponsoring a show and maybe throwing in a wee holiday to Mosney for the local radio station?' Martin said with a cheeky grin as he walked into the back office of the shop. A cup of tea and a chat later, my dad handed over the holiday voucher and cheque before adding, 'Any chance of getting my wee girl involved — she wants to work in the media?'

And that was that. Seven days later, with butterflies in my tummy, I took a deep breath and entered the Mill. 'Hi, I'm Aislinn and I am here to join the news team.' Seasoned journalist Anne Cadwallader was waiting and instantly took me under her wing. Over the next few weeks, Anne taught us the basics of radio news reporting. We learnt how to write, source and read news stories. This was long before the days of the internet, so if we needed a story we had to find it. The big day eventually came and we were ready to go on air for the first time. Sitting in the studio, the DJ pushed the news jingle button and there it was, I was live across Belfast. I never had a feeling or buzz like it and it was in that moment that I knew that when I grew up I was going to be a presenter.

In the next four weeks leading up to the Féile, the radio became our second home. We lived, breathed and basically slept there. The hours flew by as we prepared our scripts for the next hourly bulletin. We had rotas and roles. One day you were the newsreader, the next a reporter who went out to record interviews. I had never been part of a team before and I felt like this is where I belonged. The volunteers were made up of people of all ages and from all walks of life. We were an eclectic bunch but that's what made it work. For many years, I was the baby of the group. I didn't know that there was an age limit to join the team and everyone just assumed I was 16, so when they finally realised my age it was too late, I had already become part of the furniture and thankfully I was allowed to stay.

Every journalist can remember their first big interview and although mine came a little earlier than most, at age fourteen, it is still fresh in my mind. The assignment was to cover an event that Mary McAleese was attending in Clonard Monastery. I was so nervous, as I had to record the speeches and then get interviews afterwards. Double checking that my mini-disc player was fully charged, I left the station determined to do a good job; this was my big moment and I couldn't mess it up. After the ceremony, the mainstream media, such as the BBC, UTV and RTÉ, along with numerous photographers, surrounded MP Gerry Adams, hoping to get a soundbite or picture for the evening news. The next few moments I will never forget. Gerry noticed me trying to get my little microphone into the scrum. He must have seen my Triple FM press pass and told everyone to step back. He then ushered me into the middle and said he was speaking to me first and Mary McAleese followed his lead. I took out my trusty notebook, pressed play and nervously started to ask Mr Adams a few questions. The chorus of chatter filled the room 'Who is that?' 'What station is she from?' I was so proud of myself and even got a few pictures taken to mark the occasion.

You couldn't talk or write about Triple FM without mentioning our radio co-ordinator Veronica Brown, or our 'Radio Mummy' as we fondly called her. Veronica was a true inspiration and gave so many young people the support and confidence to grow. Along with her trusty right hand, Joe Begley, they pushed me each year to get more and more involved in both the radio and the overall Féile. I tried my hand at everything, from answering the phones to even driving around in the yellow Féile car with Sean Osbourne ('Flute') tuning in people's radios at home. I even helped clean the Féile marquee, which believe it or not was one of my favourite jobs, although admittedly not the most glamorous. I became good friends with the security team and bar staff. They were forever playing pranks on each other and it really was a laugh a minute.

The big turning point for me, though, was when Veronica asked me if I wanted to join *The Young Star Show*, which was made up of a group of young volunteers who played the latest chart hits and had a bit of 'craic' on air reading requests and talking about their day. I loved reading the news, but having a music show was my dream. From then I went on to present various shows over the coming years. One of the most memorable was teaming up with the Holland brothers to judge the Superstar competition. It was utter chaos, but in a good way. Showing a real love for presenting, I was put in charge of running the radio road shows which included warming up the crowds at the Féile events before various pop sensations, such as Girls Aloud and Samantha Mumba, took to the stage. This led to compering the annual Party in the Park event, which I still do today.

The radio had many homes. We left Blackstaff and moved to an old derelict bar in Conway Mill, with no windows and a few furry friends running about. It wasn't the most inspiring place to work — in fact, looking back, it was terrible — but it was ours and I spent every day there throughout the summer. We then moved to above Cooper's chemist in Andersonstown and had a few stints in the Teach na Féile before we got our new state-of-the-art radio station back in Conway Mill. This was when the radio truly evolved. We were granted our full-time license and Féile FM 103.2 was born. We had come a long way from using second-hand equipment and propping up our studio desks with CD cases. It was going to be a huge challenge; being volunteers, we now had to commit to working in the station all year round, a challenge that we all fully embraced.

Veronica sadly had to leave the station, but she left it in good hands, with Emma Mullan taking the reins. Emma was full of enthusiasm and really brought new life into the station. We became more professional, which at times we were criticised for, but we had to move with the times. And with the internet now playing a major part in our lives, the radio was able to enter a new chapter, broadcasting online across the world. It was a very exciting time.

I became the news team editor and joined the Féile management team, as well as teaming up with Tony Craig, a long-term volunteer and friend, to create *The Aislinn and Tony Show*. This was by far our most successful show and was often the station's most listened-to programme. We had people tuning in from America, Canada and Germany. It was full of fun and laughter and was the favourite part of my week. The programming schedule was bursting at the seams with exciting an innovative shows. We had presenters from the Basque Country and the Philippines, cross-community shows, slots with pensioners and young people, along with one-of-a-kind shows hosted by legends such as Basil McLaughlin and Joe Austin. There truly was something for everyone.

All good things have to eventually come to an end, and it was with a heavy heart that the station had to close its doors in 2011 due to lack of funding. I was the last person to speak on the airwaves. Holding back the tears and clearing the frog in my throat, I signed off for the very last time. Looking back now and understanding more and more — about the origins of the radio from its pirate roots, broadcasting to give our community a voice and its journey to becoming one of the biggest community radio stations in Ireland — I believe I spoke in that moment for all the volunteers, past and present, when I thanked Féile and our listeners for supporting us over the years. They gave us all so many opportunities, but more importantly many laughs and memories.

20 years on, I am still as passionate about the Féile as I was back when I was a little girl. When I think of the Féile, I think of family, friends and fun. As dramatic as it may seem, I know I would not be the person I am today if I hadn't walked up those stairs to that first radio meeting. The Féile will always have a special place in my heart for so many reasons, personal and professional. I have met the most interesting and wonderful people from all around the world and made friendships that have stood the test of time. I will always cherish my Féile memories. However, I now look forward to making new ones as we embark on a new era of Féile celebrations with a new generation of Féile staff and volunteers. And I don't know about you, but I am excited to see just how far we can go!

Realising West Belfast's tourism potential

HARRY CONNOLLY

Everyone has their own Féile story. That's the power of Féile. My Féile story is varied. I hope to capture some of it here. A daunting task. A day in Féile deserves its own memoir! Sometimes a day in Féile, outside of Féile time, is a roller-coaster of emotions, of fall-ins and fall-outs, all a day in the life!

Anyhow, here I go …

The women of the street rapped our door in Ballymurphy, collecting for the street party. A few pound a week for a rake of weeks leading into August got us kids of Divismore Park what felt like then the biggest bag of sweets ever. Divismore Park stood in the shadow of the Henry Taggart, a fortified British military installation, home to various British Army regiments and the good old RUC. Across Divismore Park lay what the older generations called 'The Green'. Ironically, it was a space covered in thick heavy concrete. We kids called it 'The Banana', a much more apt name, as it curved with the street. Anyhow, this was our space and the scene of some of the best hurling and football matches ever played in the Murph. Geordie's Housing Executive van was one net and two coats were the other. This was also the spot for our Féile street party that ran long into the evening. Our community celebrated. Despite my young age at the time, I recall a distinct political undertone to this almost defiant celebration by our wee street in the shadow of the Barracks. Although I didn't realise it then, our wee party was symbolic of what was happening across West Belfast: a resilient community celebrating.

Perhaps at the same time or a few years later, Springhill, the home of Féile entertainment, in a make-do piece of waste ground, a grey ugly space, transformed into a dynamic centre of expression through music, culture and dance that attracted people from across the city. I recall the electrical wires across the back of the stage running by extension lead into local people's homes. Local people powering the craic. We used to sneak under the fence of the newly built site and make it up to the front of the stage before we got turfed out early in

107

the evening as crowds gathered. We helped build it, hauling pieces of wood to the waste ground, up Springhill Avenue from the side of the chapel, up past Father Des Wilson's house — the community house that he developed. These were different times.

Times have changed, as has Féile. Our community and people have survived, changed and evolved with the festival. Ballymurphy has a deep level of energy, activism, sport, politics, language and critically, champions of people. Providing access to the Black Mountain and 'The Hatchy'. The Murph is the epicentre!

I worked outside of West Belfast for many years, in youth work and community development, and whilst not 'building' Féile like we did in Springhill, I always had a profound love for August time and the best memories of Féile. I reached a stage where I had missed West Belfast too much and wanted to come back and work with my own community. I was application happy — applying for any job going — and was delighted to land the co-ordinator position at Fáilte Feirste Thiar, the locally based tourism development body for West Belfast.

Shortly after taking up this post, I was invited onto the board of Féile, and felt very proud and somewhat humbled to become a board member of this extraordinary festival. The local MP's office rightly made the point that Féile and everything it represents should be joined at the hip with our tourism remit. The festival would be front and centre of a new campaign to realise West Belfast's tourism potential. We didn't just want to bring tourists here for the sake of it. We wanted to tell our story, but critically we wanted to maximise the economic and social impact of tourism for local people i.e. we wanted it to be a real catalyst for change and economic development. This had to mean local jobs for local people and new training opportunities to upskill our community to access jobs associated with the broad tourism and hospitality industry.

Féile always had an international appeal, especially amongst international activists visiting West Belfast in solidarity. This was often reflected in the various international nights that featured Corsicans, Basques and Catalans, to name a few. We took Féile on the road. We developed new relationships with statutory tourism and marketing bodies and, in Féile tradition, we lobbied to ensure that we got our fair share. We soon found ourselves taking pride of place at the world's biggest Irish festival, Milwaukee Irish Fest, promoting Féile an Phobail as Ireland's largest community arts festival to the thousands of Irish-Americans that flock to Milwaukee every August and come to Ireland in their droves.

As we approached Féile 25, a wide group of us recognised that, in order to consolidate all that Féile had achieved in the past quarter of a century, the 25th anniversary events had to be a major expression of community in all its forms. Although the days of Springhill seem long past, with the health and safety regulations well and truly in place, we nevertheless transformed our own green lung, the Falls Park, into a new event space, in the spirit of Springhill. Over the past five years this new venue has attracted a host of top music acts, catering for all genres and all tastes. Féile has succeeded in bringing world-class acts to local people at Féile value; some of these act have sold out various venues in Ireland for more than double the price of a Féile ticket. This is the power and true spirit of Féile. I'm sure that those who were in the 'Big Tent' in the park and felt the atmosphere when UB40 blasted out 'Red, Red Wine', or when we chanted with the Kaiser Chiefs' 'I Predict a Riot', were reminded, like I was, that this is what Féile is about: amazing summer nights spent in an electric environment with proud West Belfast people. Springhill didn't seem too far gone!

The debates and discussions programme has been rebranded as Ireland's Largest Summer School and is now held up as a progressive model of dialogue, debate and empowerment, attracting local people along with some of the world's leading activists and academics to explore with us national and international issues, ranging from the legacy of the recent conflict, to solidarity campaigns and topical political debates.

Not only have local people taken advantage of the festival, but also an increasing number of tourists flock to Féile. 2017 was a record year for tourism in West Belfast. The working partnership between Fáilte Feirste Thiar and Féile has opened new doors that both encompass and fulfil the Féile vision. We look forward to West Belfast's tourism potential being realised and the James Connolly Visitor Centre, Casement Park and the Roddy McCorley Visitor Attraction coming to fruition — these just some of the amazing projects that share the vision and ethos of Féile.

As Féile prepares to celebrate 30 years, our aim is to provide 'A Community Celebration of Global Culture'. That sums up Féile. Our commitment to community and inclusivity, and our dynamism as a people, are what attract visitors to our events. Happy birthday Féile — Féile abú!

Minding the jersey

KEVIN GAMBLE

1988, I was seven years old. As Féile an Phobail, Ireland's Biggest Community Arts Festival and Summer School, sets out this year to celebrate our 30th birthday, I will be 36 years old! Although to most that may (hopefully) seem young, I do feel old! The oldest of my five kids, Jude, is now seven and we are expecting number six at the end of August. When I sit back and look at what my own kids now have in front of them, and the conditions/environment in which they now live, it's hard to imagine them growing up in conditions like those back in 1988.

I am very grateful to my own parents, Bobby and Kathleen, for steering us through life. As a young boy growing up in West Belfast in the 1980s and 1990s, I remember vividly the almost daily confrontations with the police and British Army on the streets, especially at certain times of the year. I recall stories from our 'third granda', Proinsias MacAirt, about the time the British Army (SAS) had attempted to assassinate my father and his friend on the Glen Road (1978), and the time my father and he spent in prison in Crumlin Road Gaol and also in Long Kesh. There is no doubt we grew up in darker times.

When sitting down to write this short memoir, I was trying to think of my earliest Féile memory. Instead of my first thought being of an event I attended at the festival, however, I was actually drawn to one of my earliest memories as a child growing up in West Belfast — a memory that left a lasting mark, the funerals of the Gibraltar volunteers. My parents would have attended many Republican funerals over the years, and I, along with my three brothers and sister, would have been brought along. I can remember the day very clearly — the sombre mood in the community, even the tension. The anger afterwards as the news broke of people killed and injured. But as a young lad I was amazed at the huge crowds of people; everyone from the area was there. Most people reading this book will have a memory of those days, and in particular the attack on the funerals. I've no doubt that day, etched in my memory, has in part shaped the person I am today.

Some of my earliest memories are those of the street parties that almost every street throughout the West was involved in. From the collections around the doors for the food and entertainment, to hanging the bunting with rebel music blasting out, it was just a great community celebration. Little did I know there was much more to the festival, happening just down the road, with community events, political talks and debates, theatre, big concerts, sport, and a range of other activities. For me, the little street party and street games organised locally by our friends and neighbours constituted our own mini Féile.

I can remember attending some of the big concerts in both Beechmount and the marquee at the back of Westwood's shopping centre, seeing the likes of Shane MacGowan, Status Quo, and even Westlife (before they were famous) all playing at Féile! The sight and sound of screaming fans seeing their music idols playing in the heart of their local community was a great spectacle. The big concerts always generated fantastic excitement, and even when we were too young to get in 'officially', we always managed to get close enough to at least hear the gig. A club man from my own club, St Paul's, John O'Carroll, who at the time was involved in building the staging and doing security, always made sure us St Paul's lads got in.

As I was growing up in West Belfast, I always associated the festival with a time of joy and excitement in the local community, a time to relax from the trouble and strife of everyday life. After graduating from university, I was working as a sports development manager in Brownlow Sports Trust, just outside Craigavon, when an opportunity for a similar post came up in West Belfast, with the Upper Springfield Development Trust (USDT). This was a chance to work within my local community again, using sport and physical activity to regenerate local areas — an opportunity I simply couldn't turn down.

I wasn't long in post before I was encouraged to join the Féile board, to help the festival increase its sporting links and events. This was my first opportunity to see what exactly goes on behind the scenes, and I was immediately impressed with the hard work and dedication of both the staff team and the various committees and sub-committees involved in organising the festival year-round. Fast forward five years, to 2011, and the opportunity came up to apply for the main job, Director of Féile an Phobail. I can remember to this day the nerves I felt preparing for the interview; the enormity of the job dawned on me, along with the expectations. It was an opportunity to grow the festival, to take on one of the most high-profile jobs in the city. I was delighted to learn that, after a rigorous interview process, I was the successful candidate and must admit I was even more nervous after getting the job than I was applying for it.

My first week was a baptism of fire: dawn-to-dusk meetings, coordinating various sub-committees, getting to know the staff, conducting interviews with various press outlets, meeting funders and stakeholders, and just throwing myself in at the deep end. I was supported immensely during this time by our then chairperson, Danny Morrison, and by other Féile stalwarts, including Ciarán Kearney, Angela Mervyn, Sam Baker and Harry Connolly.

Before deciding to apply for the job, I was aware of a sense within the local community that Féile had somewhat lost its edge — lost its connection to, or appeal for the local community. I was determined to reconnect the festival with local 'hearts and minds', and alongside the board, immediately started thinking of ways to re-establish the festival with the community at our centre. I also felt that a whole new generation of young people were growing up with no real connection or appetite to engage with the festival programme. And so we set about developing a new vision for the 'relaunching' of Féile, locally, nationally and internationally. I will come back to this shortly.

I remember my first big public event as Director — The Stranglers, live in Andersonstown Leisure Centre sports hall. With around 800 fans screaming for their idols to come on stage, I was backstage taking it all in when Danny Morrison said to me 'you're up kid'. I had a nervous excitement running though me as I was introduced on stage as the new Féile Director. My job was to introduce the headline act to a screaming audience. I can't even remember what I said, but it was a first taste of the anticipation and excitement that Féile brings each year to this community. It was a proud moment for me, and it was this first 'on-stage' experience that started me thinking about transforming the entertainment element of the festival, moving it to a bigger stage, attracting more top artists and bringing in even bigger audiences. And so the dream to develop the Falls Park into a Féile HQ festival site was started.

This also brought forward a range of initiatives aimed at relaunching the festival and capturing the public's imagination again. Over the next five to six years, along with a dedicated board and entertainment committee, we worked to transform the Féile concert experience, moving from a local leisure centre holding 800-1000 people to a purpose-built accessible event space, at the Falls Park, in the heart of West Belfast, welcoming world-class artists with audiences of up to 10,000-15,000.

As well as our entertainments committee, the festival also has a range of other dedicated committees, all made up of volunteers giving up their time and working throughout the year to ensure we deliver a festival the community can be proud of: our community engagement committee, youth arts committee, events committee, and the longest serving committee of the festival, the Debates and Discussions (D&D) committee. I must say that I have not known a more dedicated committee than the D&D committee, previously chaired by Danny Morrison and now with Emeritus Professor Bill Rolston at the helm. They meet on a weekly basis year-round to produce perhaps the aspect of the programme that most put Féile on the map — our debates and discussion programme, with over 60 events each year, covering topics from local to international politics, and issues such as health and well-being, policing and justice, and much, much more. This annual series is now known as Ireland's largest summer school.

As with all of the highs of being the Director of Féile, there are also some very challenging periods I have experienced during my time — funding cuts, power outages during big gigs, flooding of festival sites, non-appearances of artists/speakers; most, simply hazards of the job. One occasion that perhaps sticks out more than others was the reaction we received when we booked the comedian Frankie Boyle to headline the festival's comedy night. While we were aware that he often courts controversy with some of his comedy, it's fair to say we did not anticipate some of the local community's negative reaction towards the booking due to remarks he made against people with Down Syndrome. Although this was the fastest-selling Féile gig ever, and to some a huge success (it sold out in a matter of days), the negative reaction and fall-out was a deep regret.

After listening to some of the people campaigning against the gig, it was clear to myself and to the Féile Board that we had not fully considered the potential reaction to the booking, and although we consulted with the protesting group, with hindsight it is something that I would have liked to have handled better. The majority of those protesting were from the local community, all with genuine concerns, some of them friends and former team mates of mine and others members of the board also, so it was a difficult position for everyone to be in. If it can be said that anything positive came out of the experience, it was that it focused our minds more on the bookings we were making, right across the festival, and the possible community impact they could have. I suppose with a job of this type, and the types of events we organise, right across the many art forms, we are always going to encounter challenges and resistance, some warranted, some not; but all provide opportunities to learn and adapt.

Alongside my team, I am proud and honoured to have played a small part in the progress and growth of the festival, and whatever the future holds, I believe that Féile will forever remain a beacon of hope and purpose for our community, and for other communities coming out of conflict around the world. While the direction and style of the festival will no doubt change in the future, the purpose will always remain the same. Since becoming Director almost seven years ago now, I have learned along the way, and continue to learn, the great benefits the festival has brought to this community, not only in terms of the economic boost, but also in terms of social enrichment, community cohesion, local tourism and community access to the arts. The role the festival has played and continues to play in developing and embedding the peace and progress we have experienced this last twenty-plus years is significant too. We have withstood everything those who would like to see us fail can throw at us, and as a community we have endured, we have grown, we have celebrated, and importantly, we have played our part in building a better future.

I remember reading a book about why the All Blacks are so successful, and one of the many credits to their success was their 'sense of purpose' — 'minding the jersey', as they put it. What makes our festival special, is our sense of purpose: our festival is very much there for the people, a true festival of the people. My job, and that of those currently working or volunteering for the festival is simply to 'mind the jersey' and ensure we leave it in a better place for those coming behind us to take up that challenge.

Often people ask me who my favourite person was to come to Féile, or did I get my photo with this or that person. To me — and I honestly mean this — it has never been about the big names. Alongside the blood, sweat, toil and tears, my best memories, and the photos that stand out the most to me, are those showing people laughing, having fun, remembering the past, and celebrating the future — those are the memories that last forever! I have made some friends for life during my time at the festival. That's what Féile is and should always remain about — the community.

In the darkness of 1988, and the years leading up to that period, an idea was born. Those visionary community leaders who initiated the very first Féile, and those that have carried the torch to date, have ensured our community is on the world map, expressing ourselves, showcasing our love and passion for the arts, for language, for sport and for community, celebrating who we are and welcoming the world to come and visit. As I mentioned at the start of this short memoir, I was seven years old back when Féile was born in 1988, in a dark, challenging time for this community. As we look forward to celebrating the 30th birthday of the festival this August, the eldest of my kids will be seven, and while we still face many challenges, I look forward, with them, and with pride in West Belfast, to a bright future for this community, and to the next 30 years of Féile an Phobail.